MY DOG'S
THE WORLD'S BEST DOG

By Suzy Becker

WORKMAN PUBLISHING, NEW YORK

In memory of
Esther Whitcomb
1901 - 1995

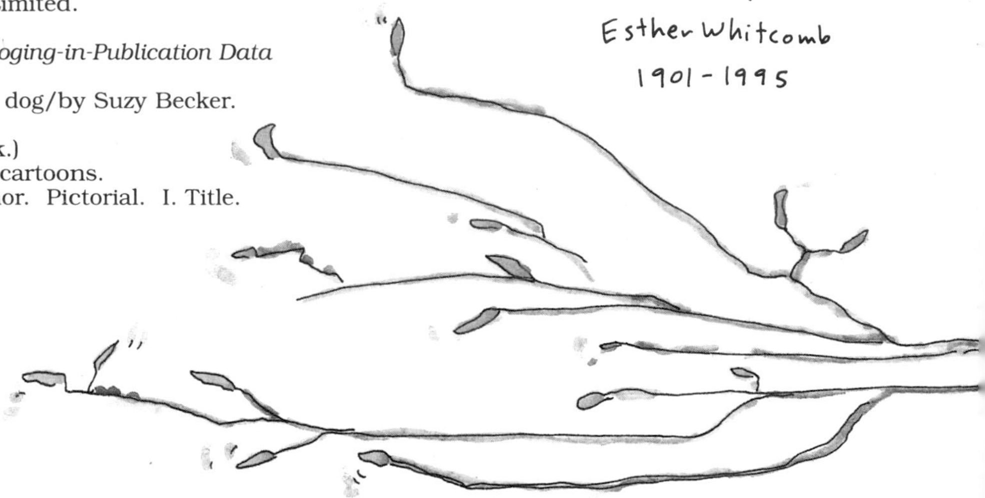

Library of Congress Cataloging-in-Publication Data
Becker, Suzy
My dog's the world's best dog/by Suzy Becker.
p. cm.
ISBN 0-7611-0105-5 (pbk.)
1. Dogs–Caricatures and cartoons.
2. American wit and humor. Pictorial. I. Title.
NC1429.B3515A4 1995
741.5`973-dc20

95-34378
CIP

Workman Publishing
708 Broadway
New York, NY 10003

Manufactured in the United States of America

First printing September 1995

10 9 8 7 6 5 4 3 2 1

MY DOG'S THE WORLD'S BEST DOG

FOR

MEREDITH, ROBIN

and the love of WYLIE...

with special thanks to: EDITE, SALLY
KATHY, AMY, NANCY and the rest
at WORKMAN.

MY DOG COMES FROM A LONG LINE OF VERY FINE DOGS.

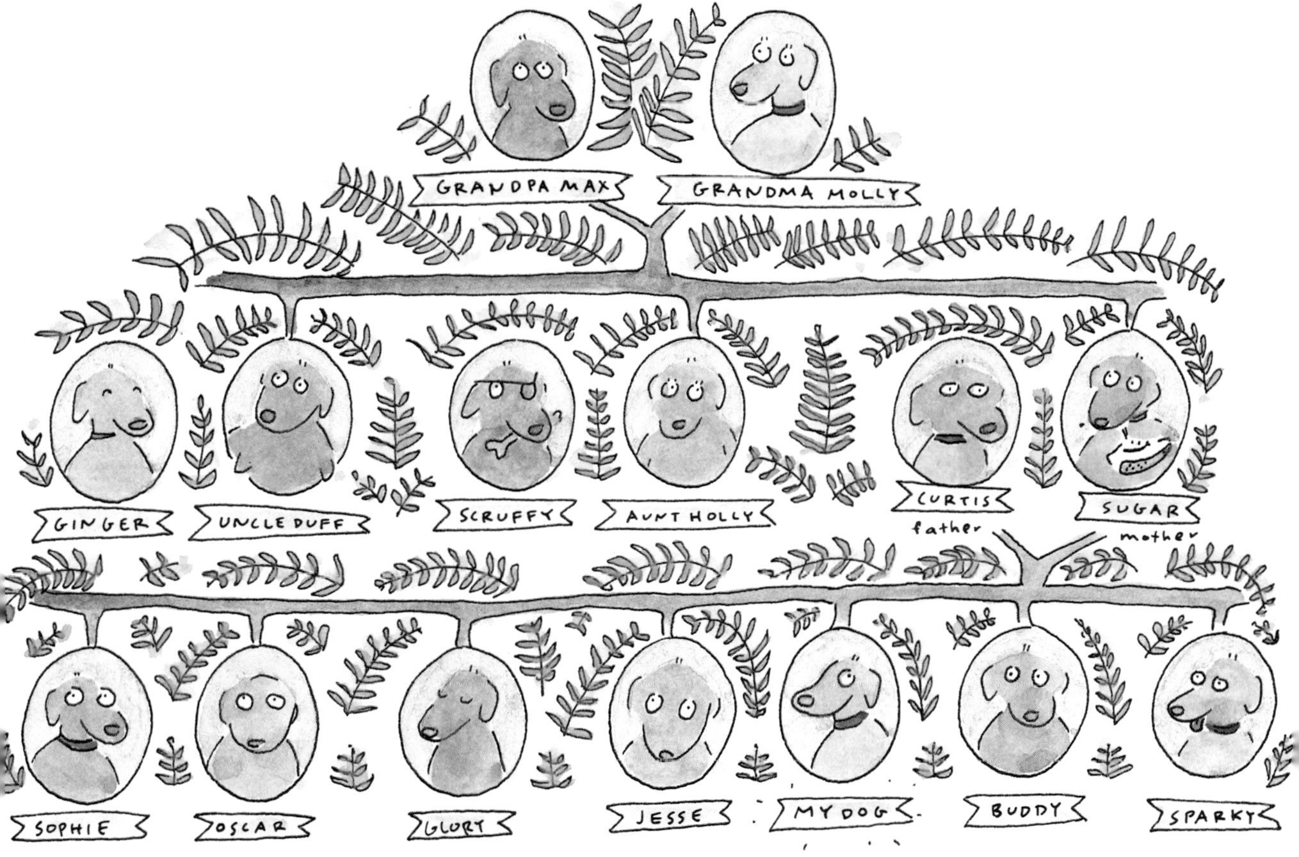
GRANDPA MAX
GRANDMA MOLLY
GINGER
UNCLE DUFF
SCRUFFY
AUNT HOLLY
CURTIS
father
SUGAR
mother
SOPHIE
OSCAR
GLORY
JESSE
MY DOG
BUDDY
SPARKY

SHE WAS THE CUTEST PUPPY...

AT FIVE WEEKS
YOU COULD ALREADY SEE SHE WAS GOING TO HAVE
A LOT OF PERSONALITY.

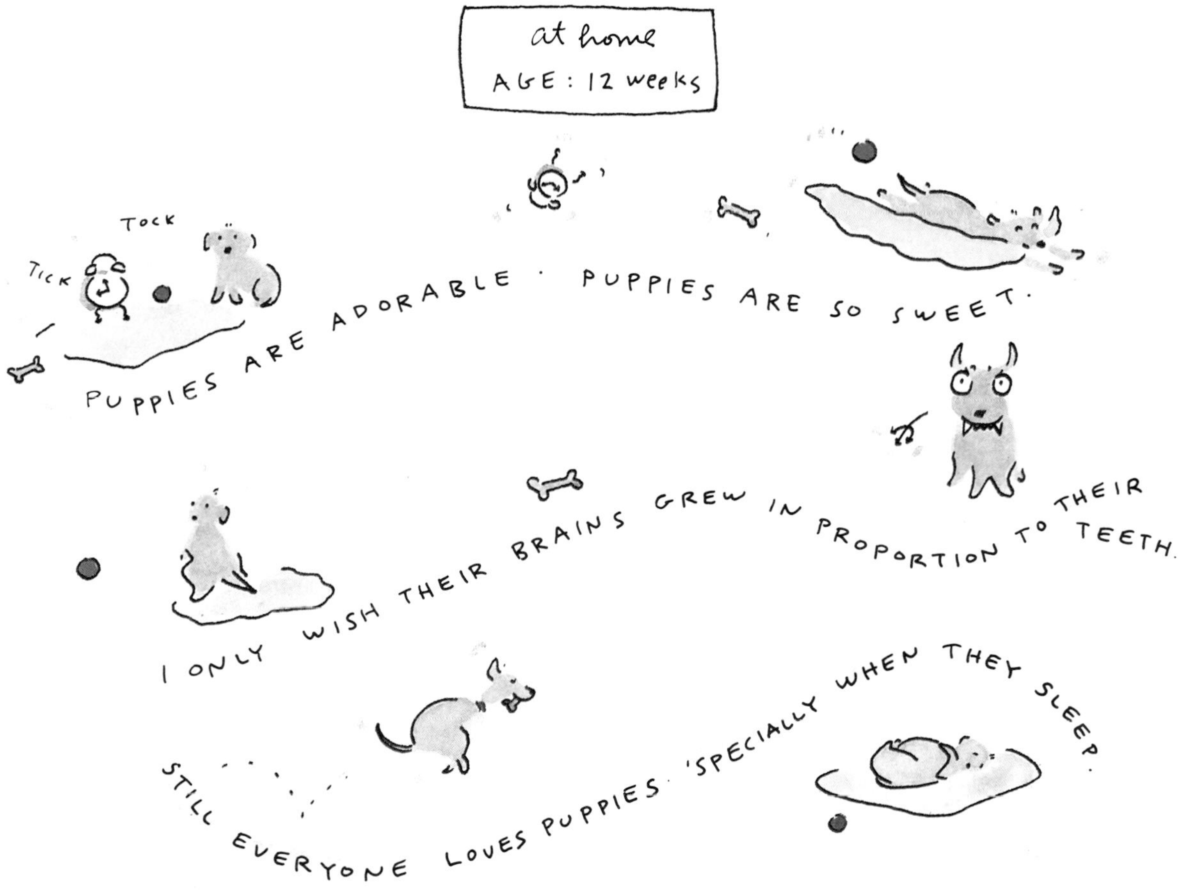
at home
AGE: 12 weeks
TICK
TOCK
PUPPIES ARE ADORABLE. PUPPIES ARE SO SWEET.
I ONLY WISH THEIR BRAINS GREW IN PROPORTION TO THEIR TEETH.
STILL EVERYONE LOVES PUPPIES. 'SPECIALLY WHEN THEY SLEEP.

THE CORNER

PEOPLE TELL YOU THAT YOUR DOG'LL TURN A CORNER AT SIX MONTHS, BUT IT TURNS OUT TO BE MORE LIKE ELEVEN, EXCEPT IN SPECIAL CASES WHERE THE CORNER WILL FOREVER BE JUST AROUND

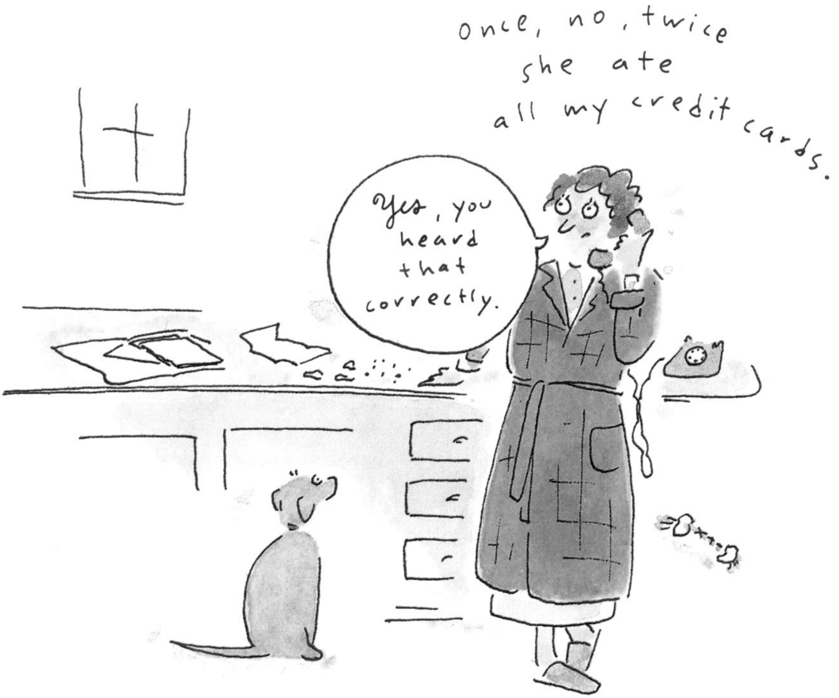

WE ENROLLED IN PUPPY SCHOOL RIGHT AWAY.

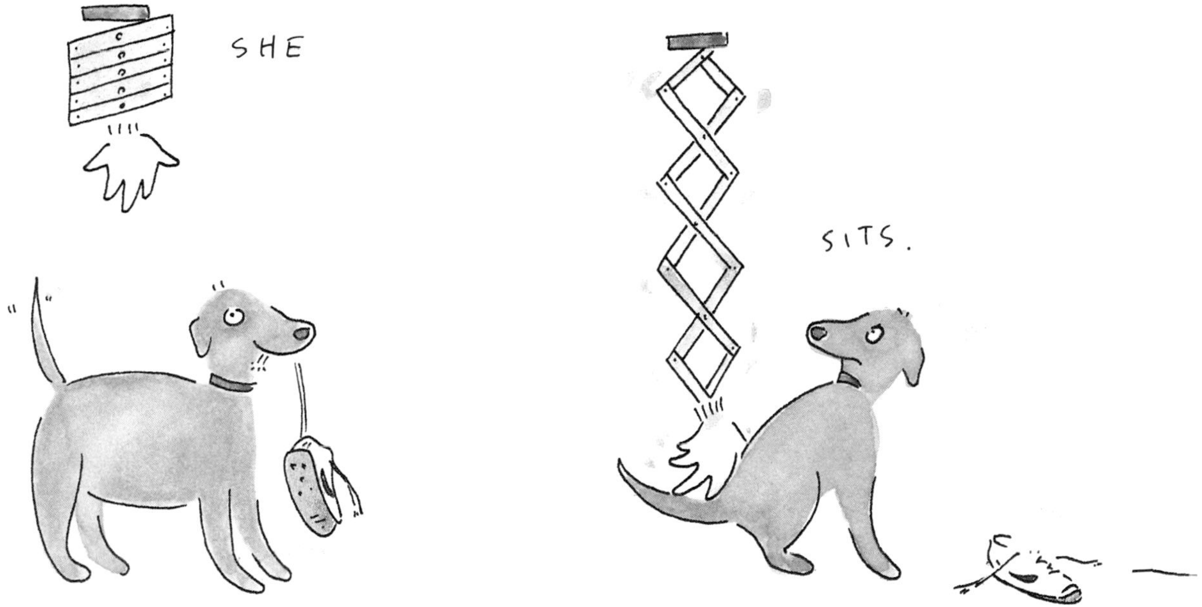
SHE
SITS.

SHE STAYS.

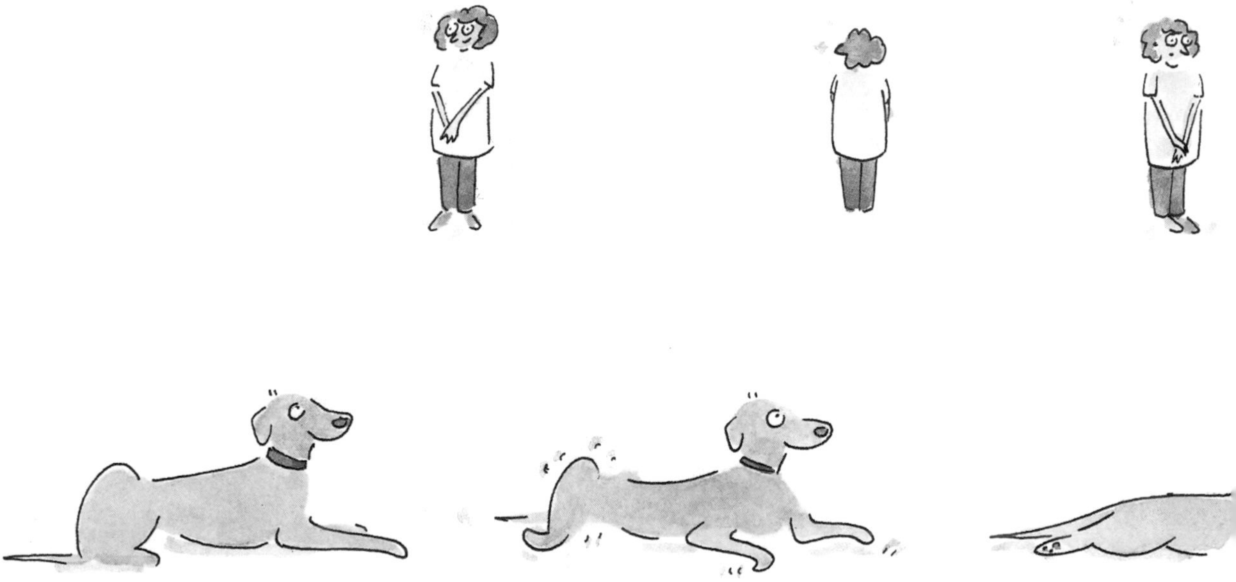

SHE JUMPS UP less.

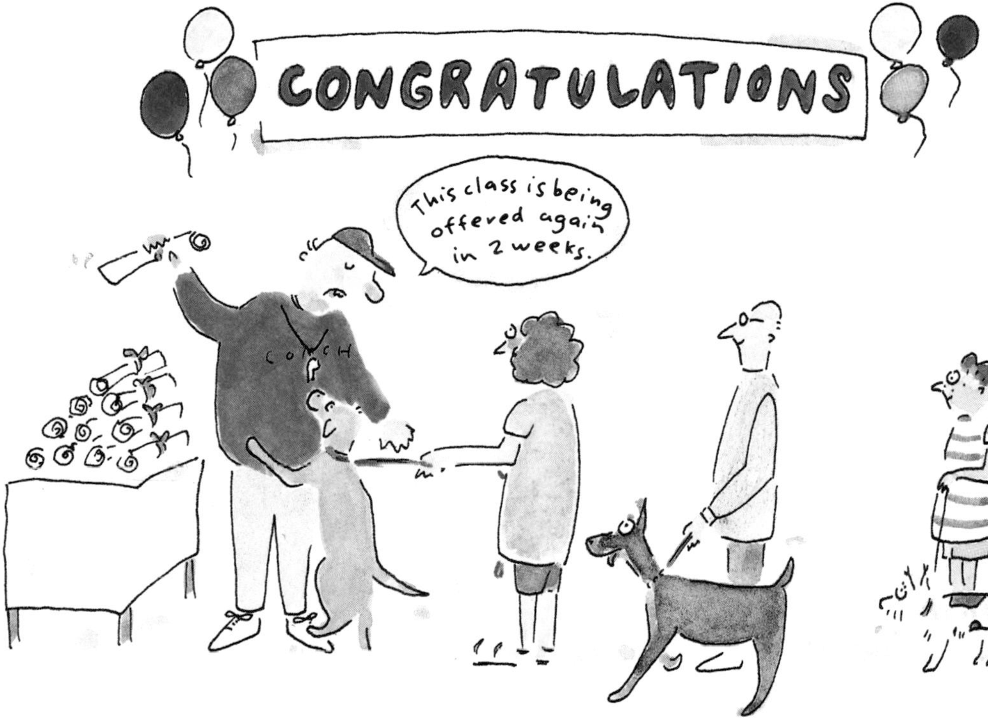
CONGRATULATIONS
This class is being offered again in 2 weeks.

TOTAL STRANGERS STOP TO COMPLIMENT ME ON MY DOG.

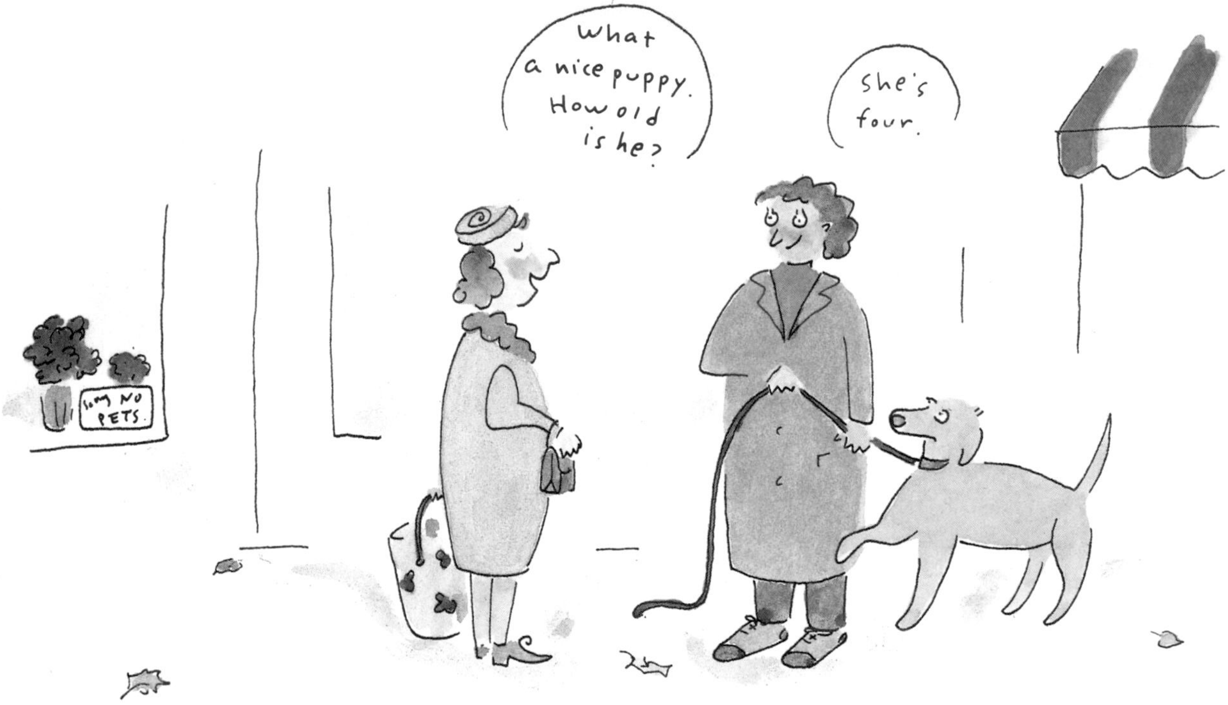
What a nice puppy. How old is he?
She's four.
NO PETS.

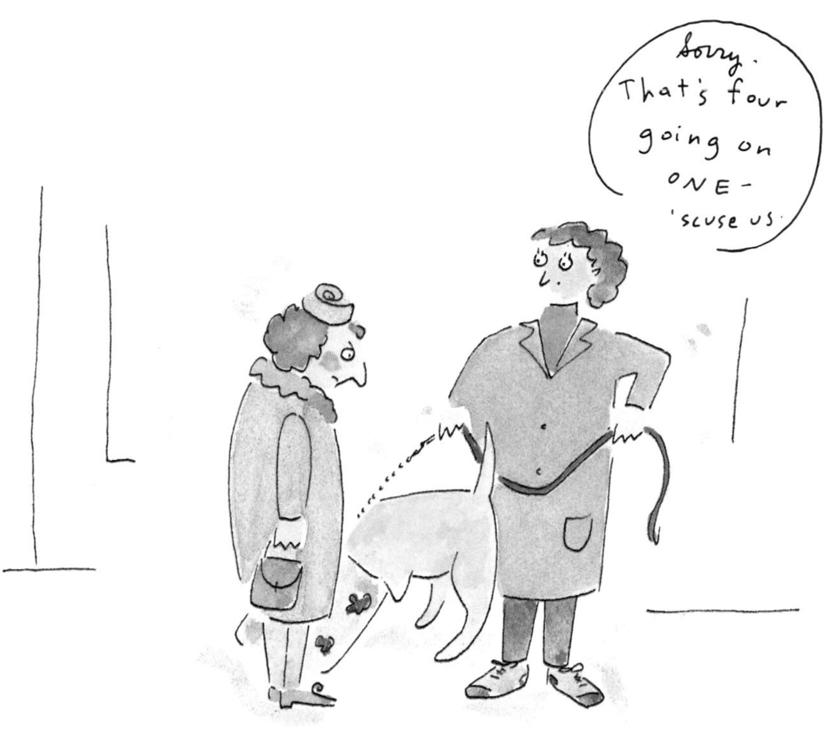
Sorry. That's four going on ONE- 'scuse us.

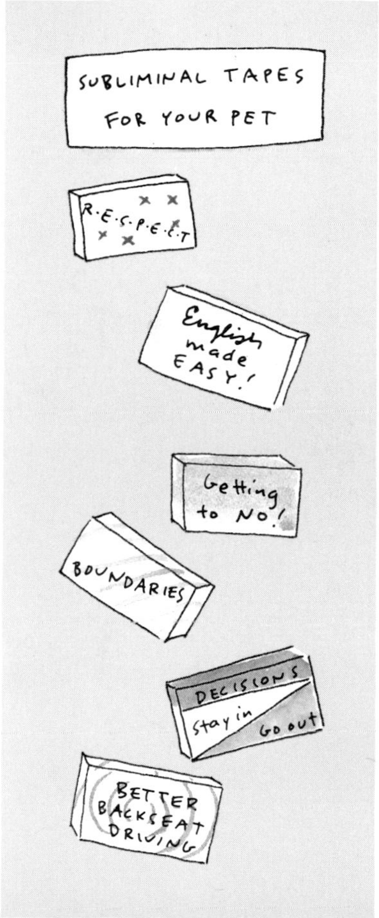
SUBLIMINAL TAPES FOR YOUR PET
R.E.S.P.E.C.T
English made EASY!
Getting to NO!
BOUNDARIES
DECISIONS
Stay in
Go out
BETTER BACKSEAT DRIVING

SHE *IS* A VERY GOOD-LOOKING DOG
WITH A *naturally* LUSTROUS COAT.

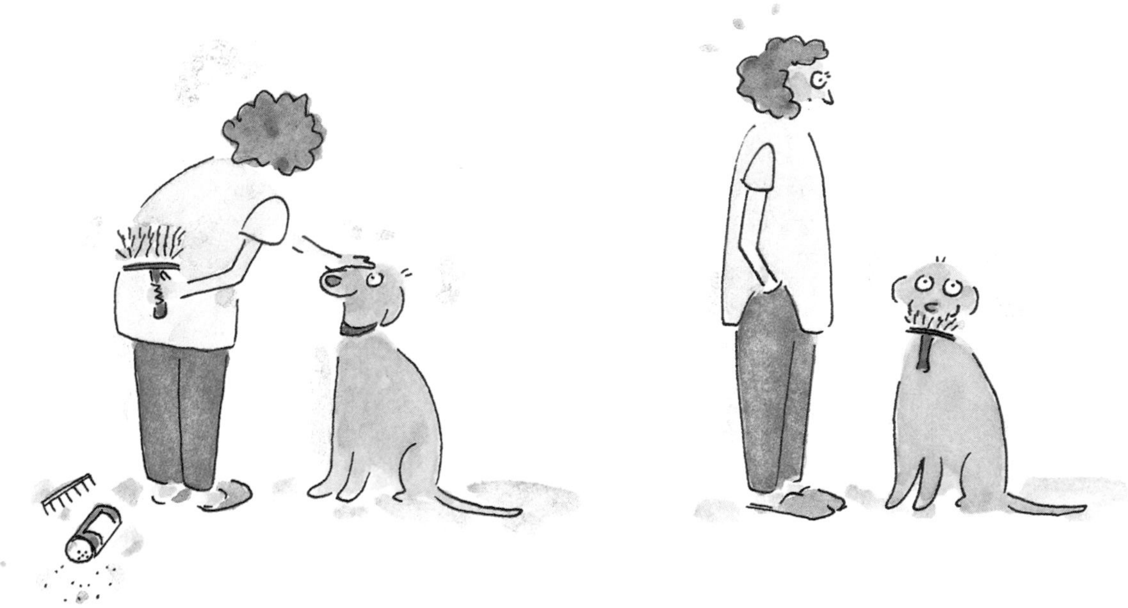

Personal RULE OF THUMB: I do not spend more time on my pet's grooming than my own.

I'VE NEVER HAD TO TRIM HER NAILS.

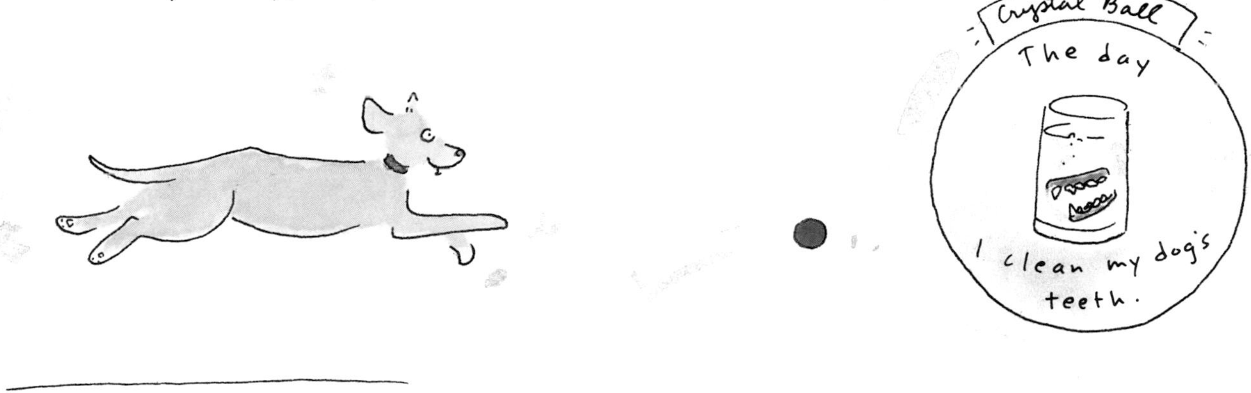

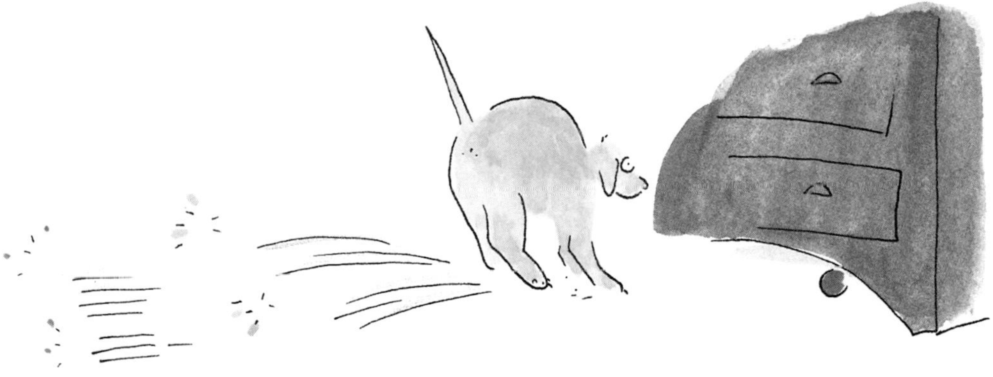

GOOD NEWS!

They now have bottled water for pets ...who have long demonstrated their distaste for water on tap by drinking:

BAD NEWS: This flavor is not even being test-marketed.

I AM VERY STRICT WITH HER DIET.

what I feed her

(Absolutely no people food.)

FANCY PREMIUM Fresh Frozen
ʒ ₵ ₵ ʒ
AND lots of it

3 cups daily

Bottomless Dish

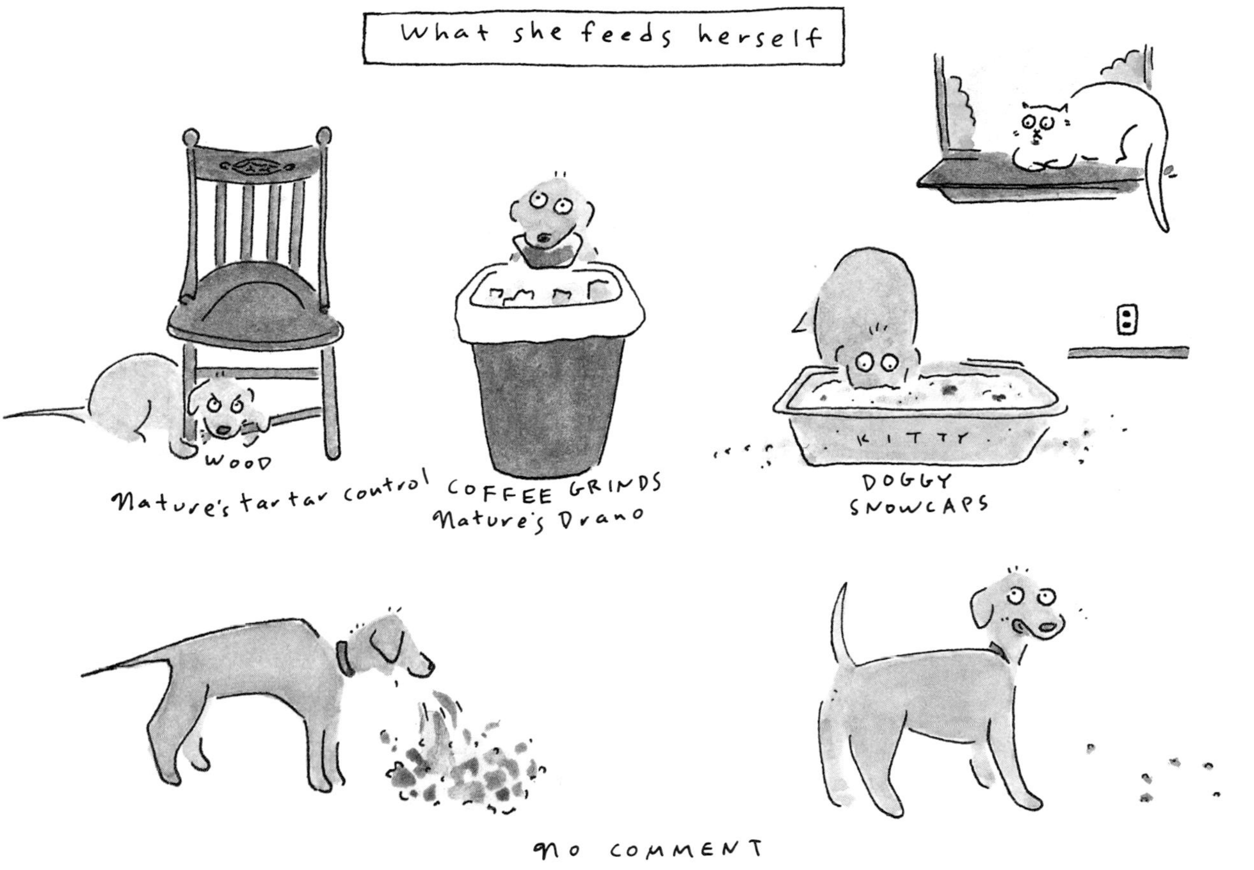
What she feeds herself
WOOD
Nature's tartar control
COFFEE GRINDS
Nature's Drano
KITTY
DOGGY
SNOWCAPS
No COMMENT

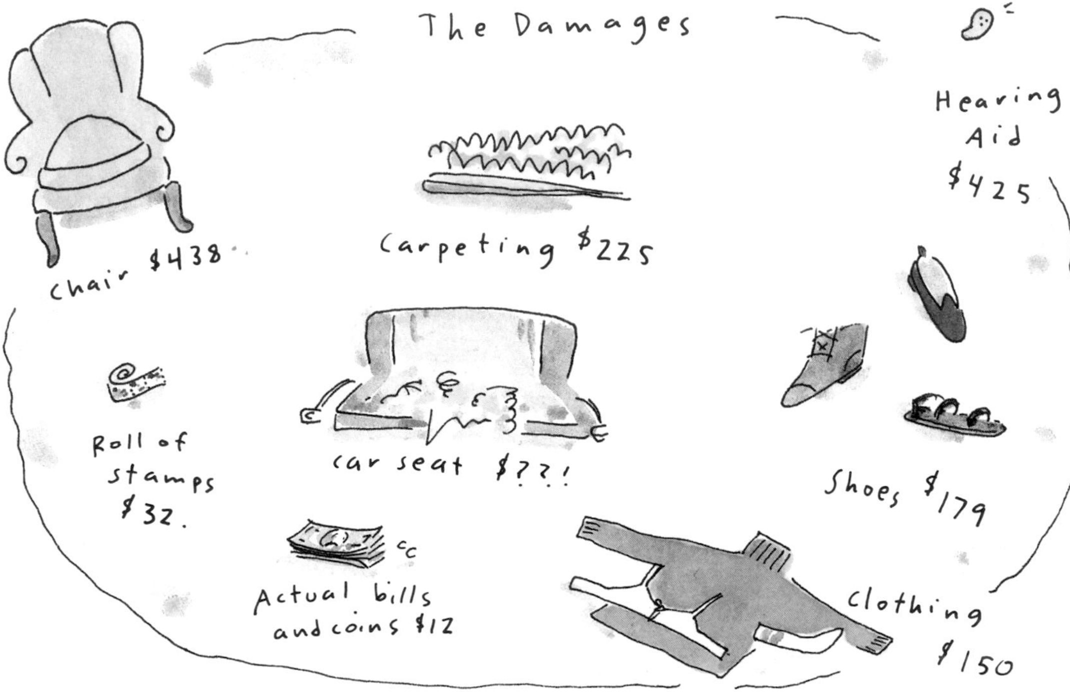
The Damages
chair $438
Carpeting $225
Hearing Aid $425
Roll of stamps $32.
car seat $??!
Shoes $179
Actual bills and coins $12
Clothing $150

(YOU CANNOT PUT A PRICETAG ON LOVE.)

SHE DOESN'T CHEW THINGS UP ANYMORE

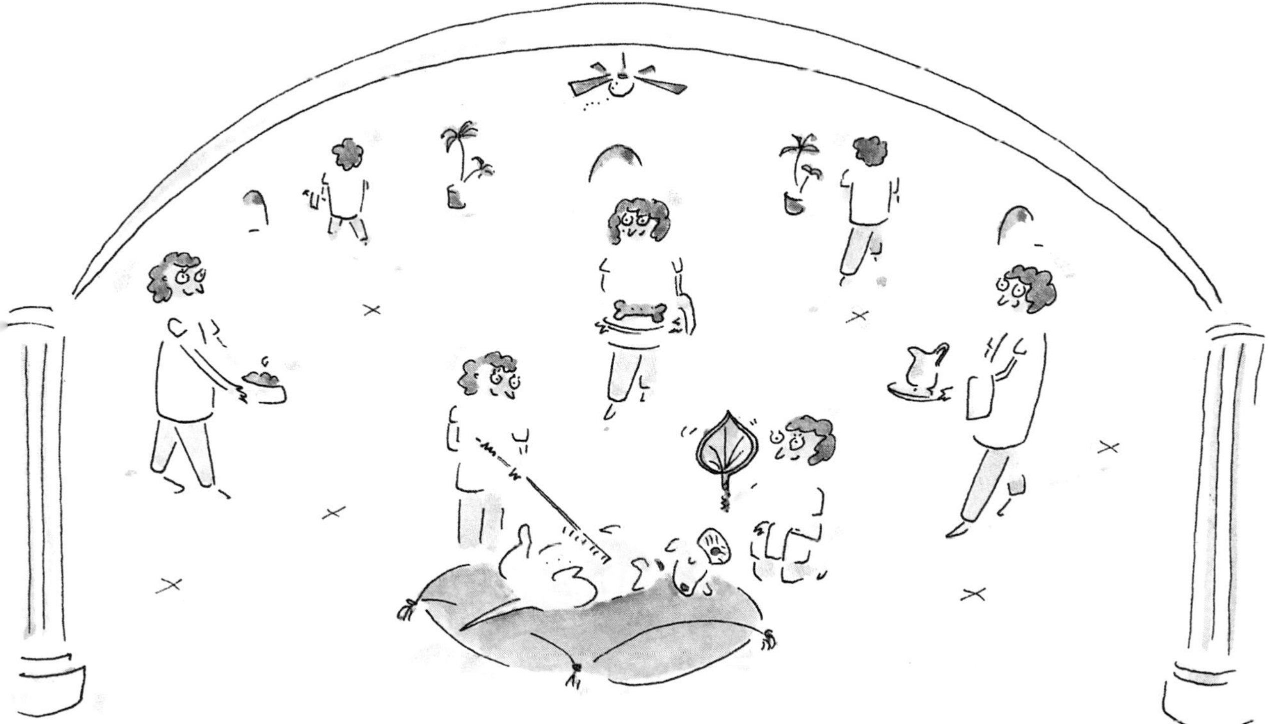

as long as she's getting enough attention.

FYI: #1. MY DOG IS *not* FAT.

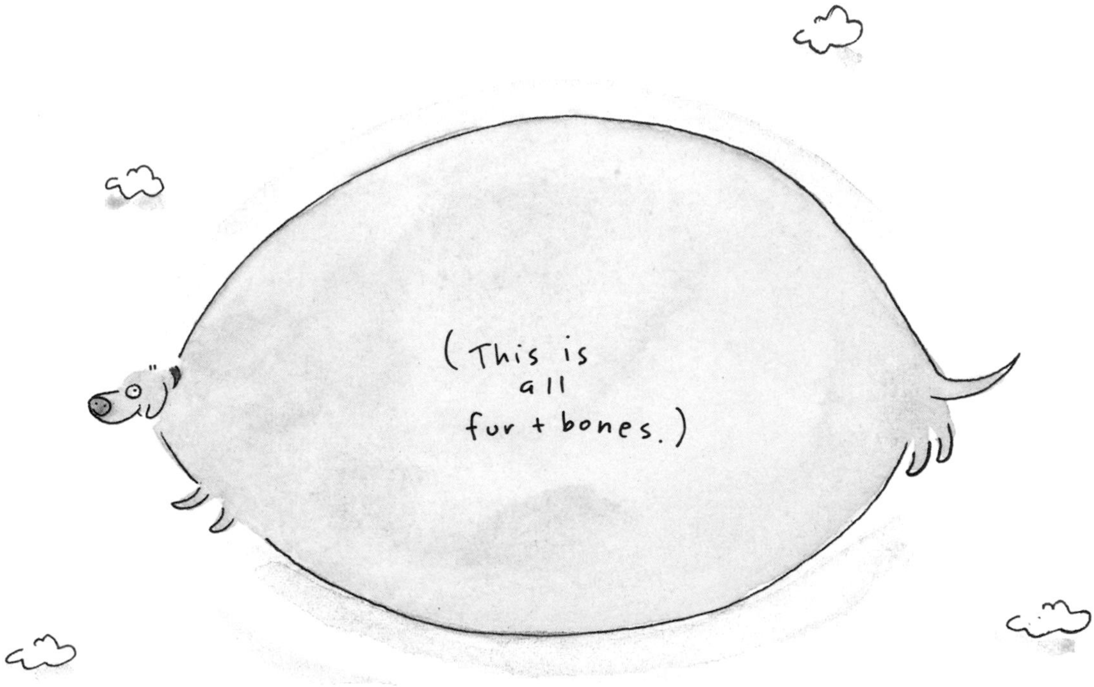
(This is all fur + bones.)

2. SHE DOES <u>not</u> HAVE BAD BREATH.

AND #3 — I AM <u>not</u> SENSITIVE ABOUT 1 or 2.

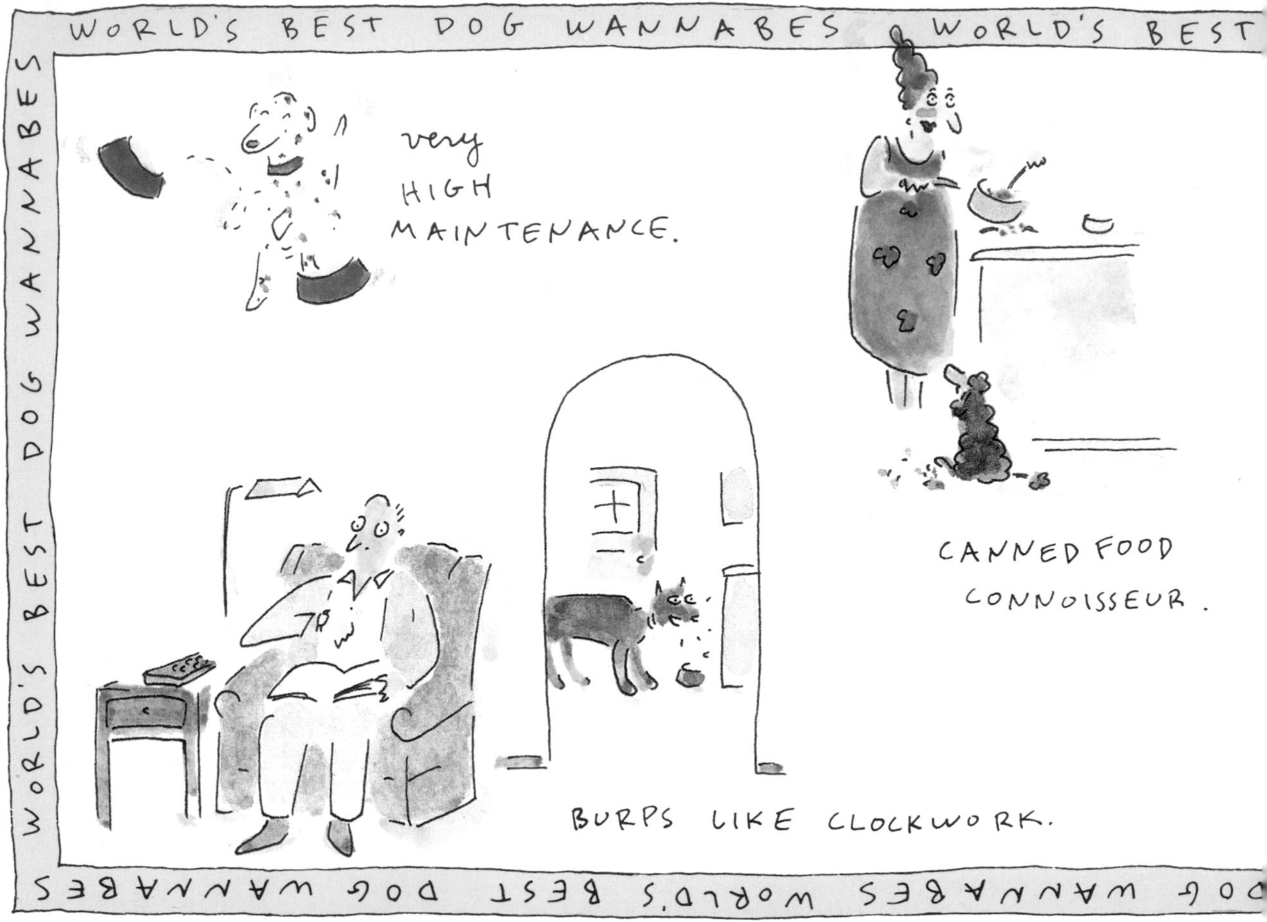
WORLD'S BEST DOG WANNABES • WORLD'S BEST
WORLD'S BEST DOG WANNABES
very HIGH MAINTENANCE.
CANNED FOOD CONNOISSEUR.
BURPS LIKE CLOCKWORK.
DOG WANNABES WORLD'S BEST DOG WANNABES

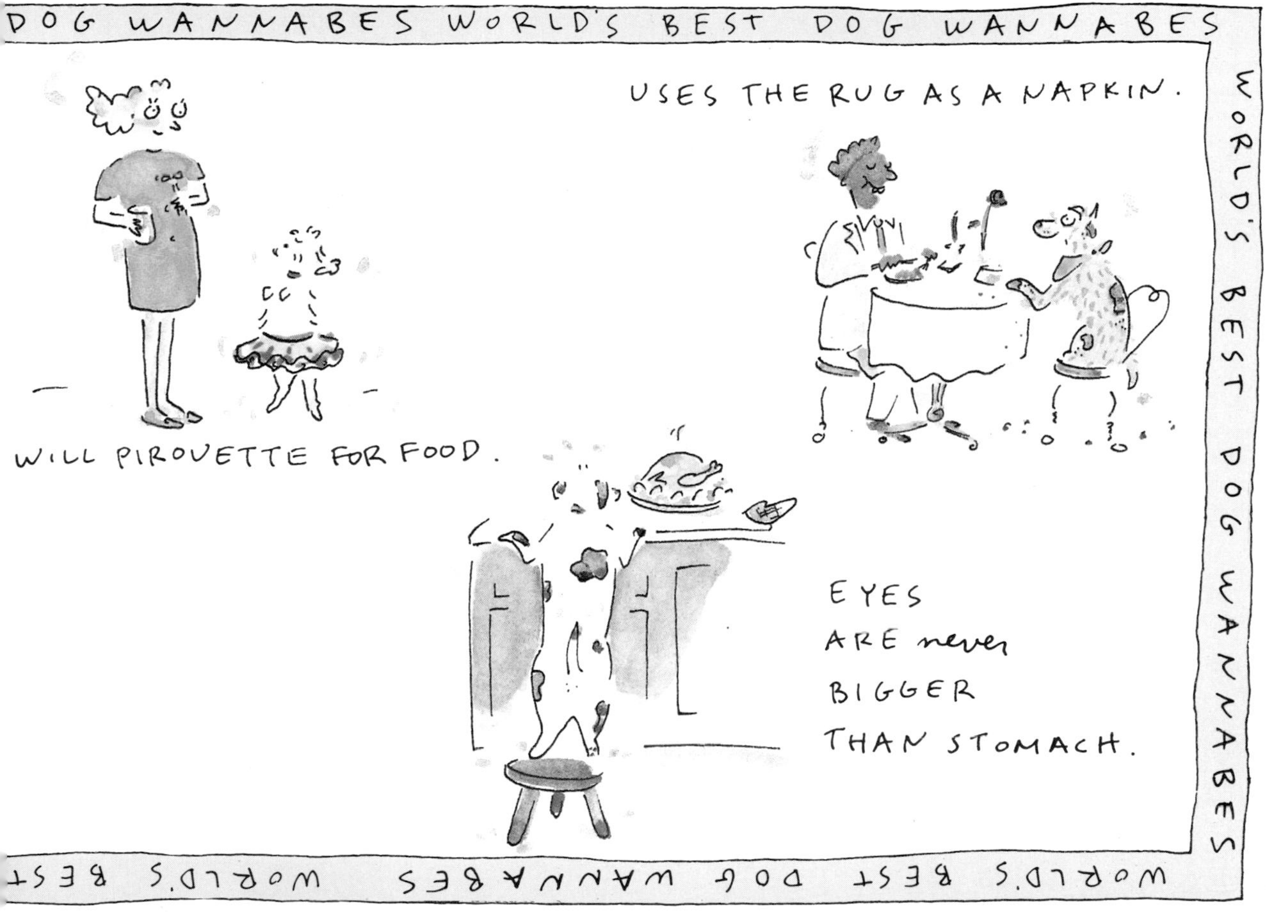
DOG WANNABES WORLD'S BEST DOG WANNABES
WILL PIROUETTE FOR FOOD.
USES THE RUG AS A NAPKIN.
EYES ARE never BIGGER THAN STOMACH.
WORLD'S BEST DOG WANNABES
WORLD'S BEST DOG WANNABES WORLD'S BEST

MY DOG'S A RETRIEVER. SHE FETCHES...

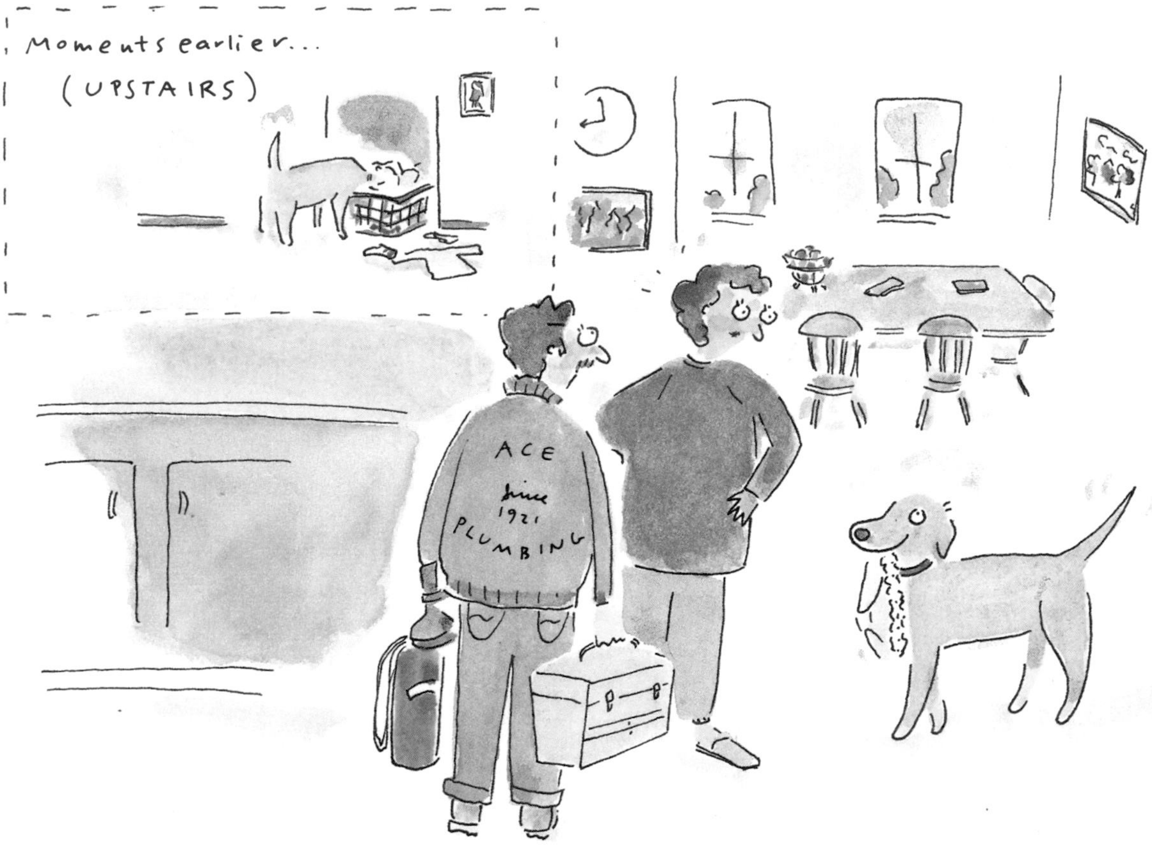
Moments earlier...
(UPSTAIRS)
ACE
Since
1921
PLUMBING

AND CATCHES.

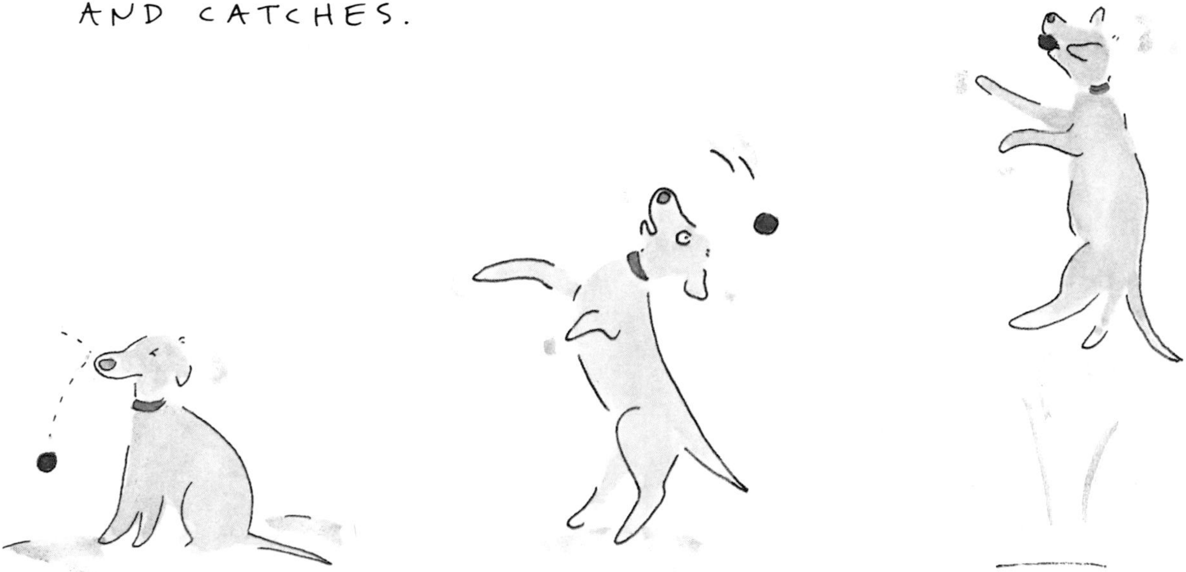

RELEASE IS really
COMING ALONG.

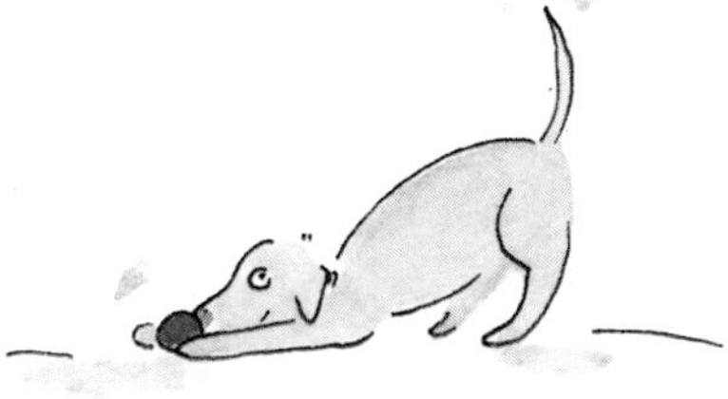

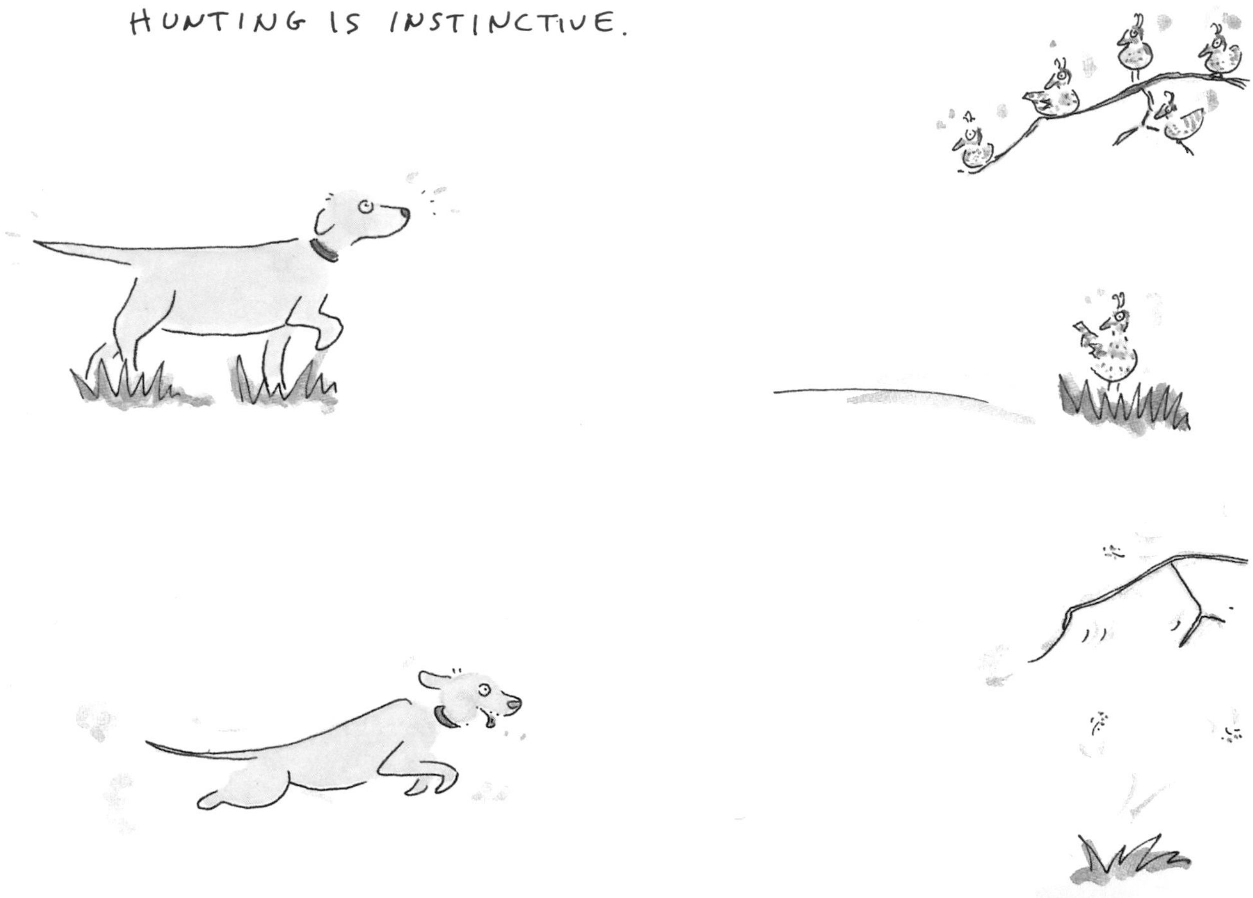
HUNTING IS INSTINCTIVE.

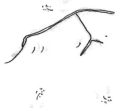

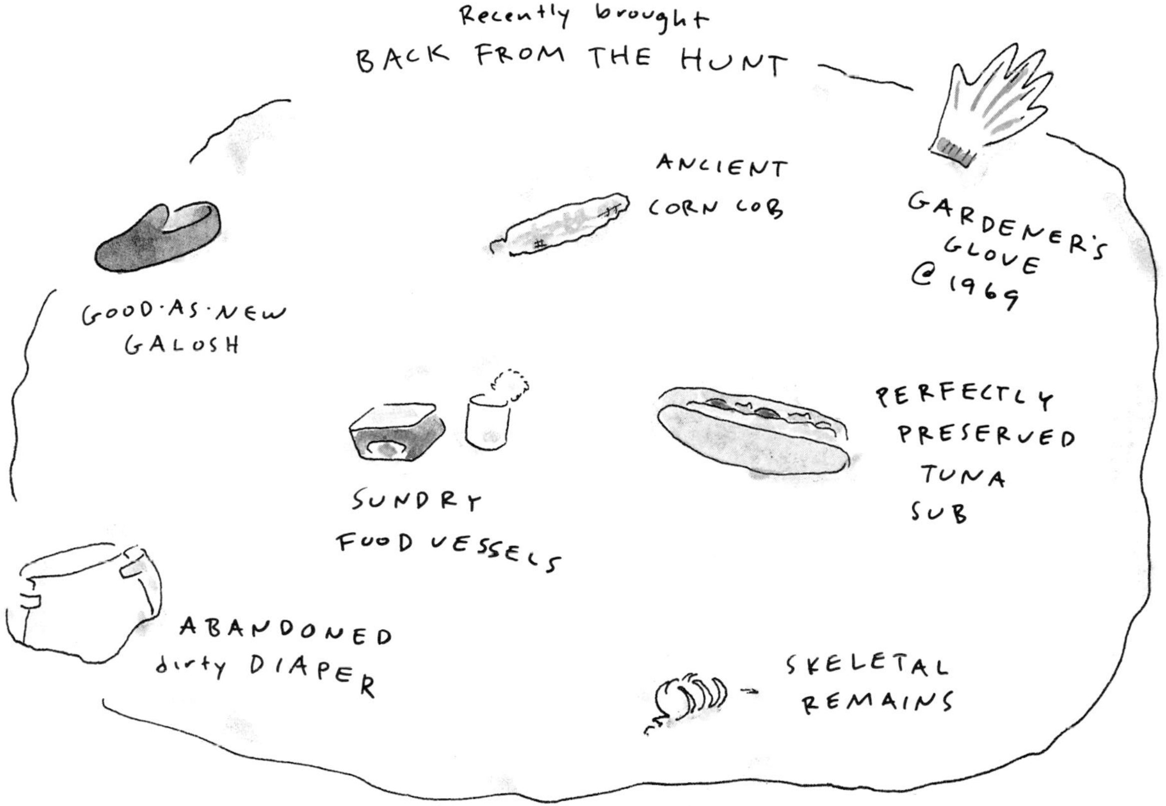
Recently brought
BACK FROM THE HUNT
ANCIENT CORN COB
GARDENER'S GLOVE @ 1969
GOOD·AS·NEW GALOSH
SUNDRY FOOD VESSELS
PERFECTLY PRESERVED TUNA SUB
ABANDONED dirty DIAPER
SKELETAL REMAINS

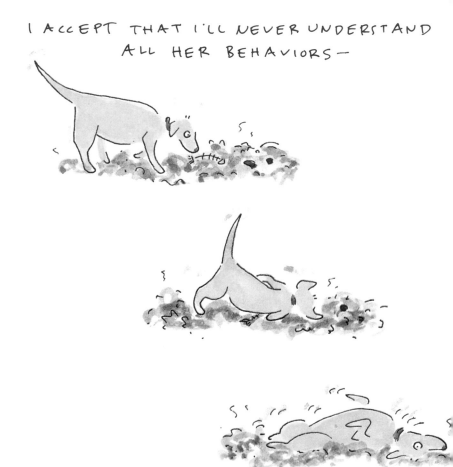

SCIENTIFIC EXPLANATION

Descendants of wolves, dogs will roll in odoriferous substances, transferring the scent to the right shoulder. The scent is said to create a favorable impression among other pack members.

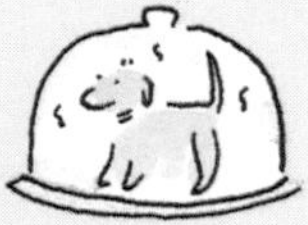

MY PERSONAL OBSERVATION

Other dogs are NOT impressed.

I ACCEPT THAT I'LL NEVER UNDERSTAND ALL HER BEHAVIORS—

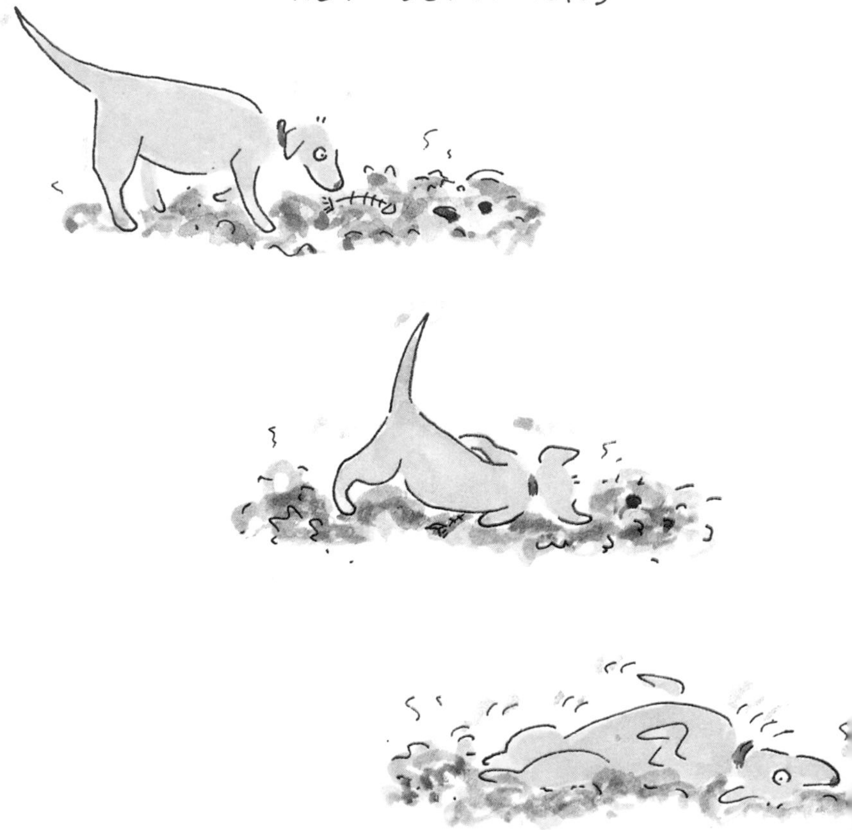

AND SHE DOES THE SAME FOR ME.

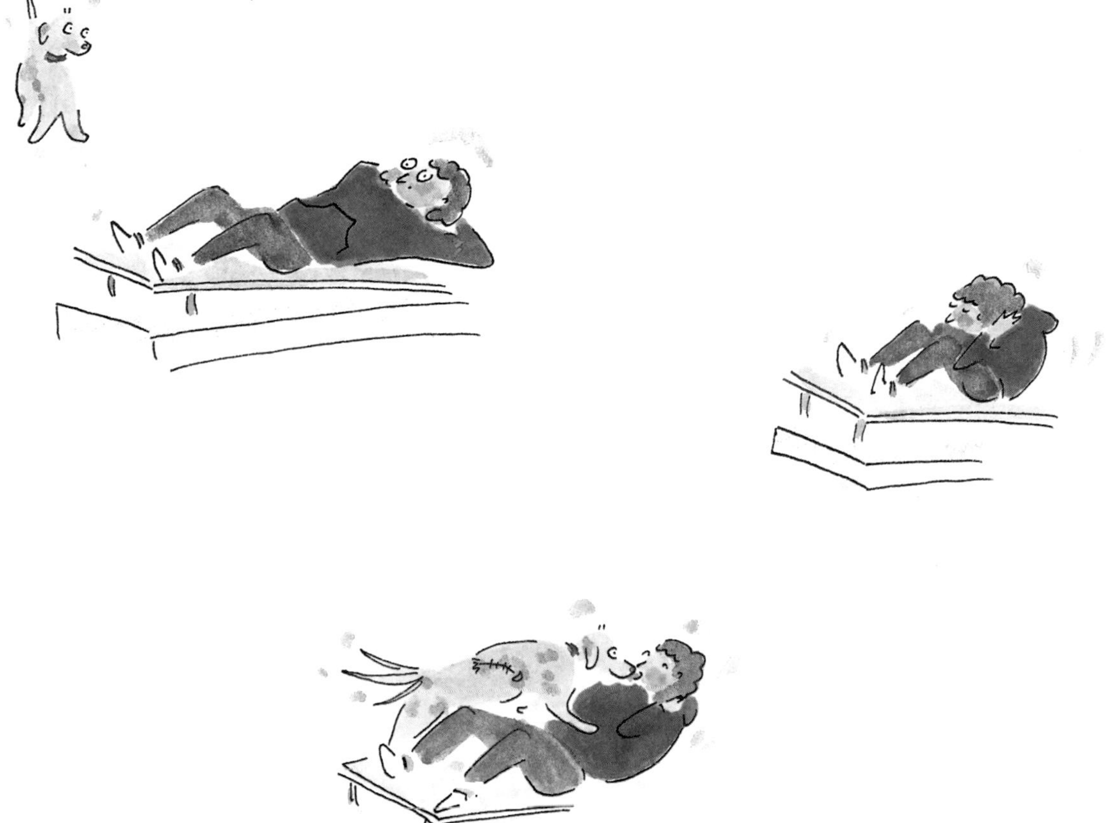

MY DOG'S A REGULAR DIVINING ROD.

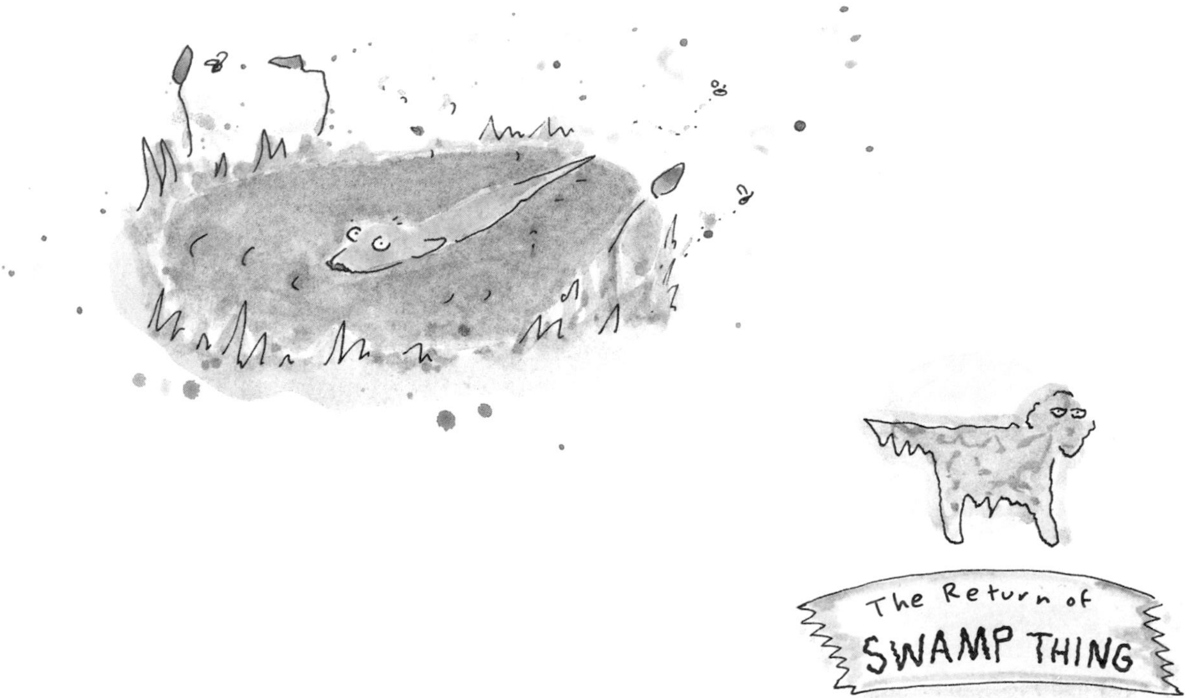
The Return of
SWAMP THING

SHE LOVES THE WATER...

The Running Dive

The Classic Paddle

. . . AS LONG AS IT'S *not* IN THE BATHTUB.

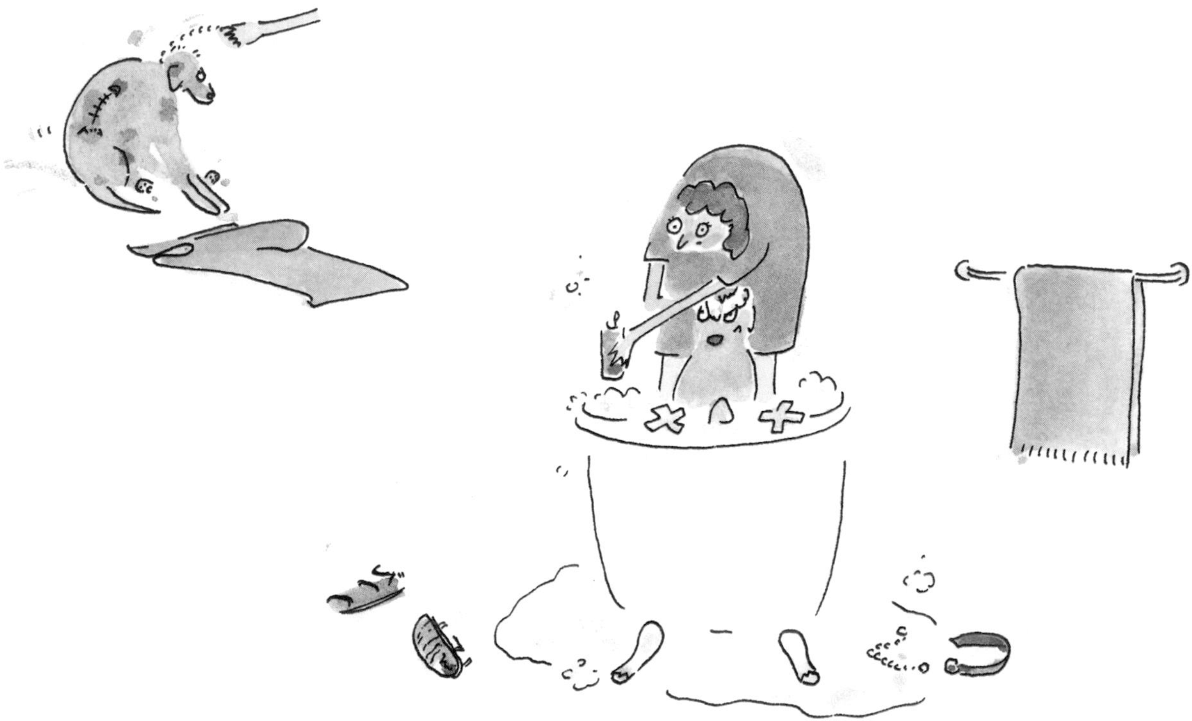

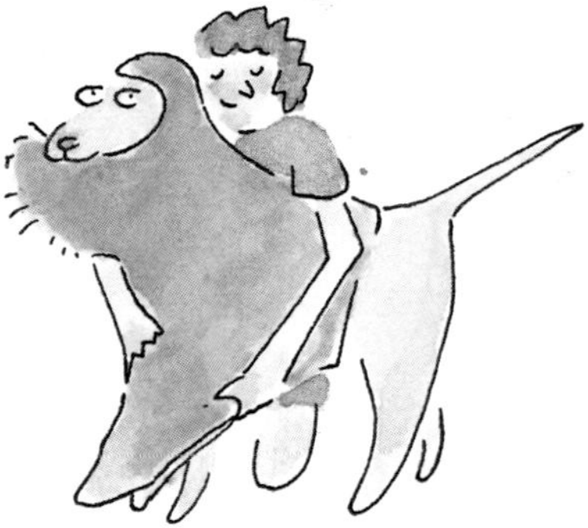
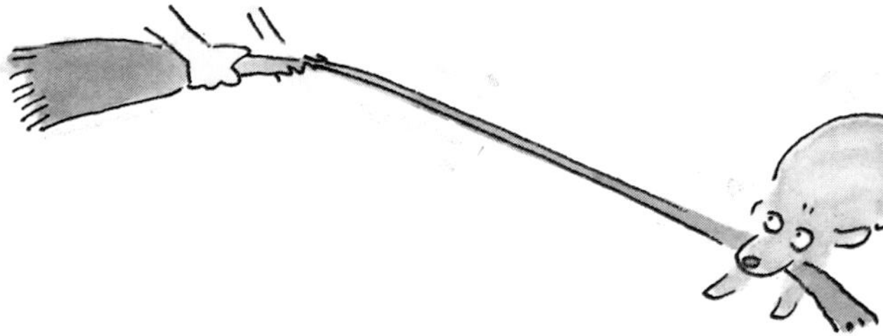
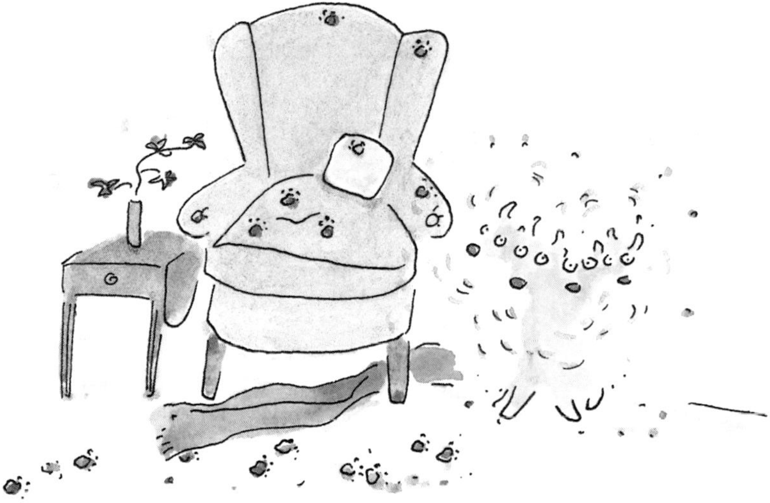

MY DOG HAS A BIG BARK and no bite.

Exhibit A NOTHING

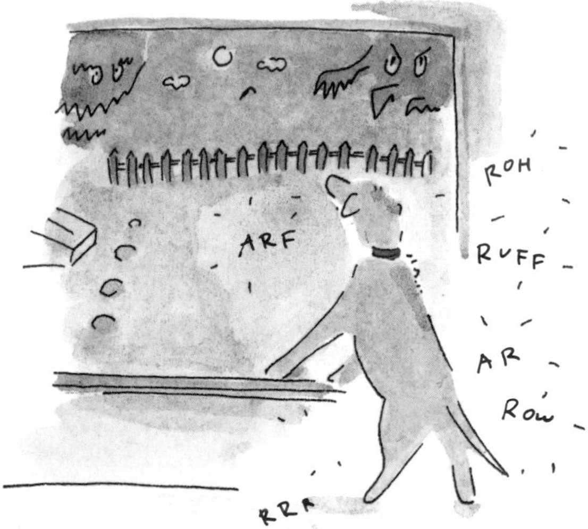
ROH
ARF
RUFF
AR
Row
RRR

Exhibit B STRANGER

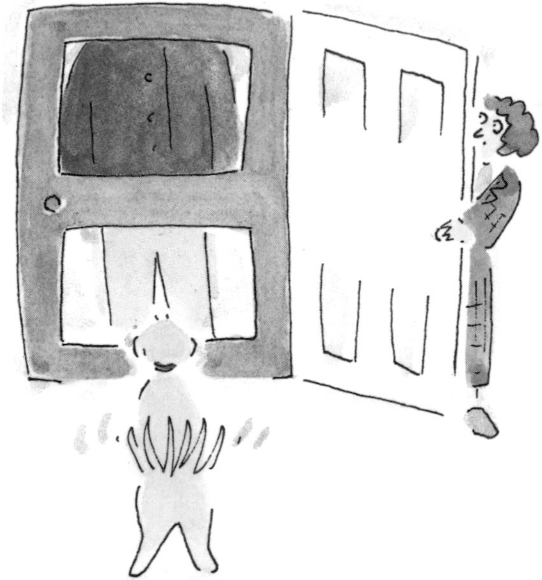

Exhibit C MOTHER and her little dog

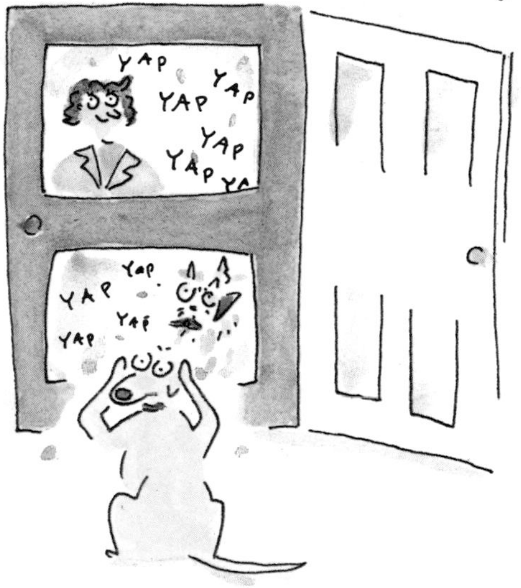
YAP
YAP
YAP
YAP
YAP
YAP
Yap
YAP
YAP
YAP

THE WATCHDOG BACK SHUFFLE

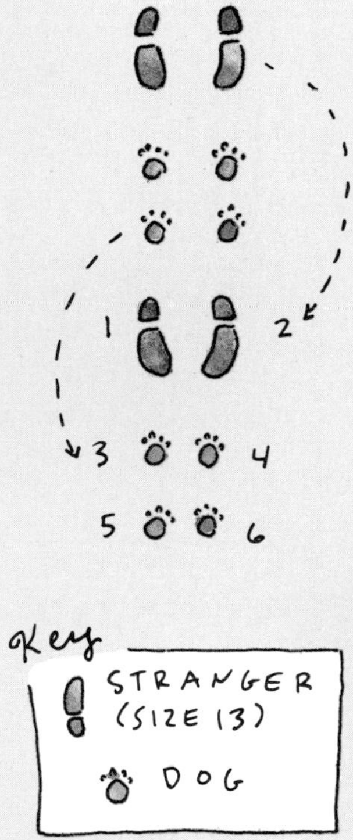
1
2
3
4
5
6
Key
STRANGER (SIZE 13)
DOG

MY DOG'S THE MODEL HOSTESS.

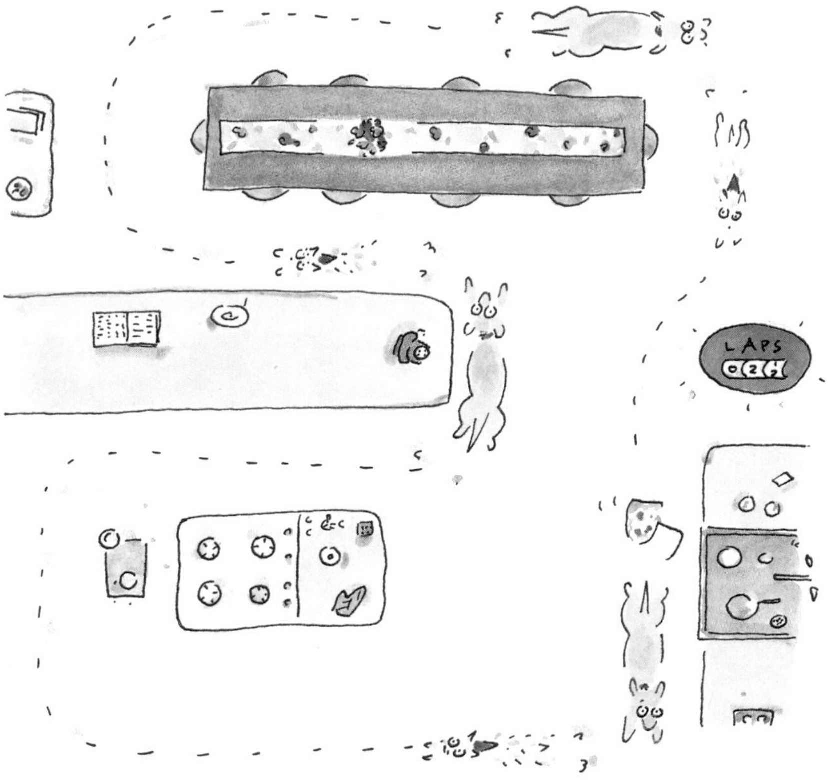
LAPS

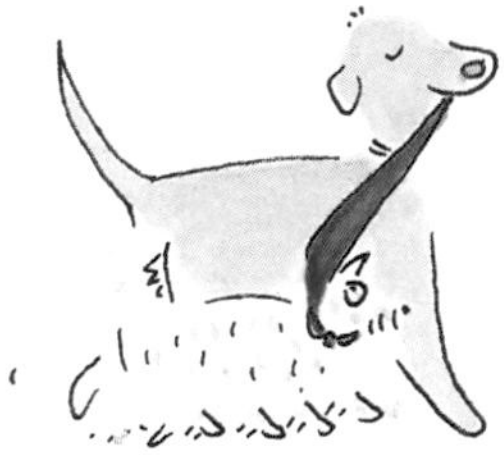

SHE ENTERTAINS THE LITTLE ONE,

ATTENDS TO THE FOOD,

AND SPENDS QUALITY TIME
WITH THE GUEST OF HONOR.

I NEVER SAID

SHE HAD THE WORLD'S BEST MANNERS.

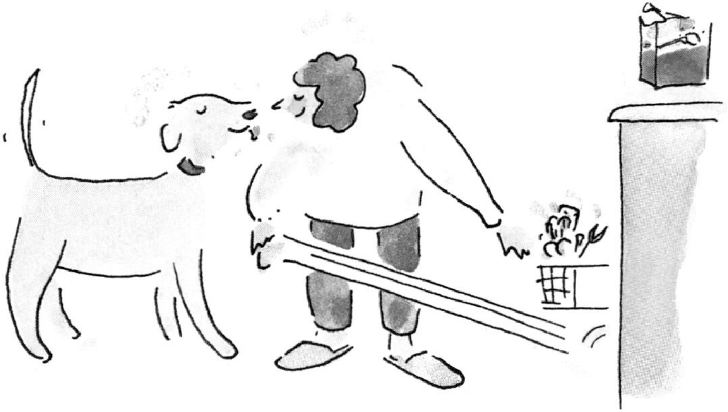

She's the World's Best Dog.

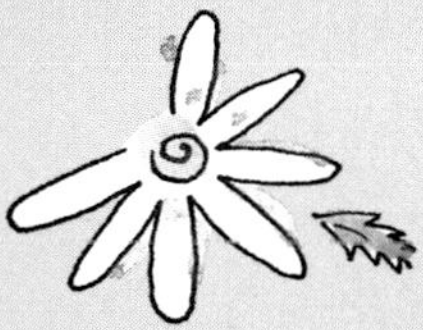

She LOVES

ME . . .

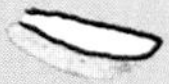

She LOVES

THE FOOD

ON MY FACE.

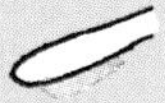

She LOVES

ME . . .

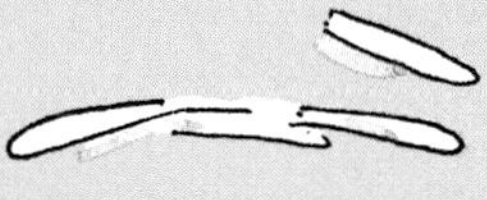

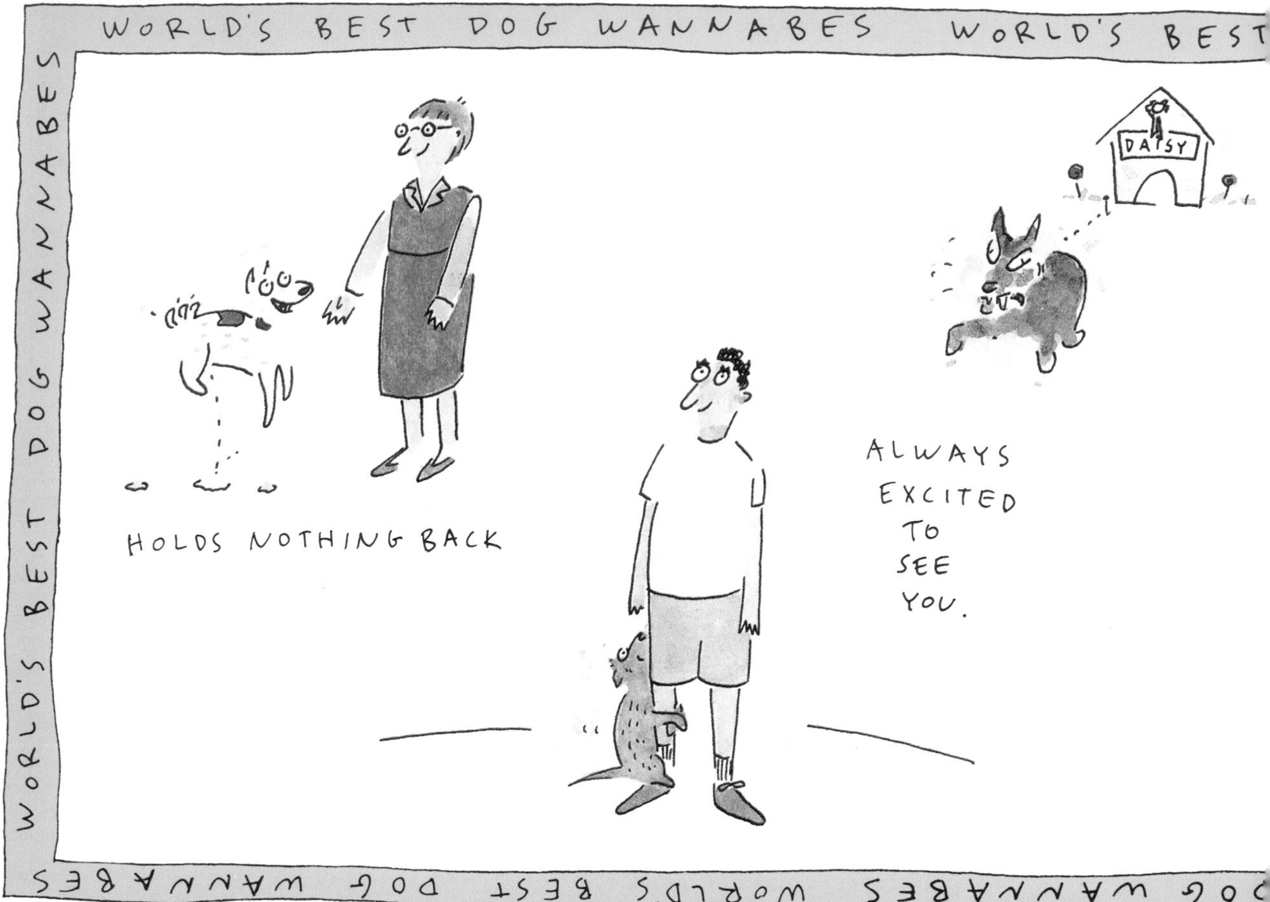
WORLD'S BEST DOG WANNABES WORLD'S BEST
WORLD'S BEST DOG WANNABES
WORLD'S BEST DOG WANNABES
HOLDS NOTHING BACK
DAISY
ALWAYS EXCITED TO SEE YOU.

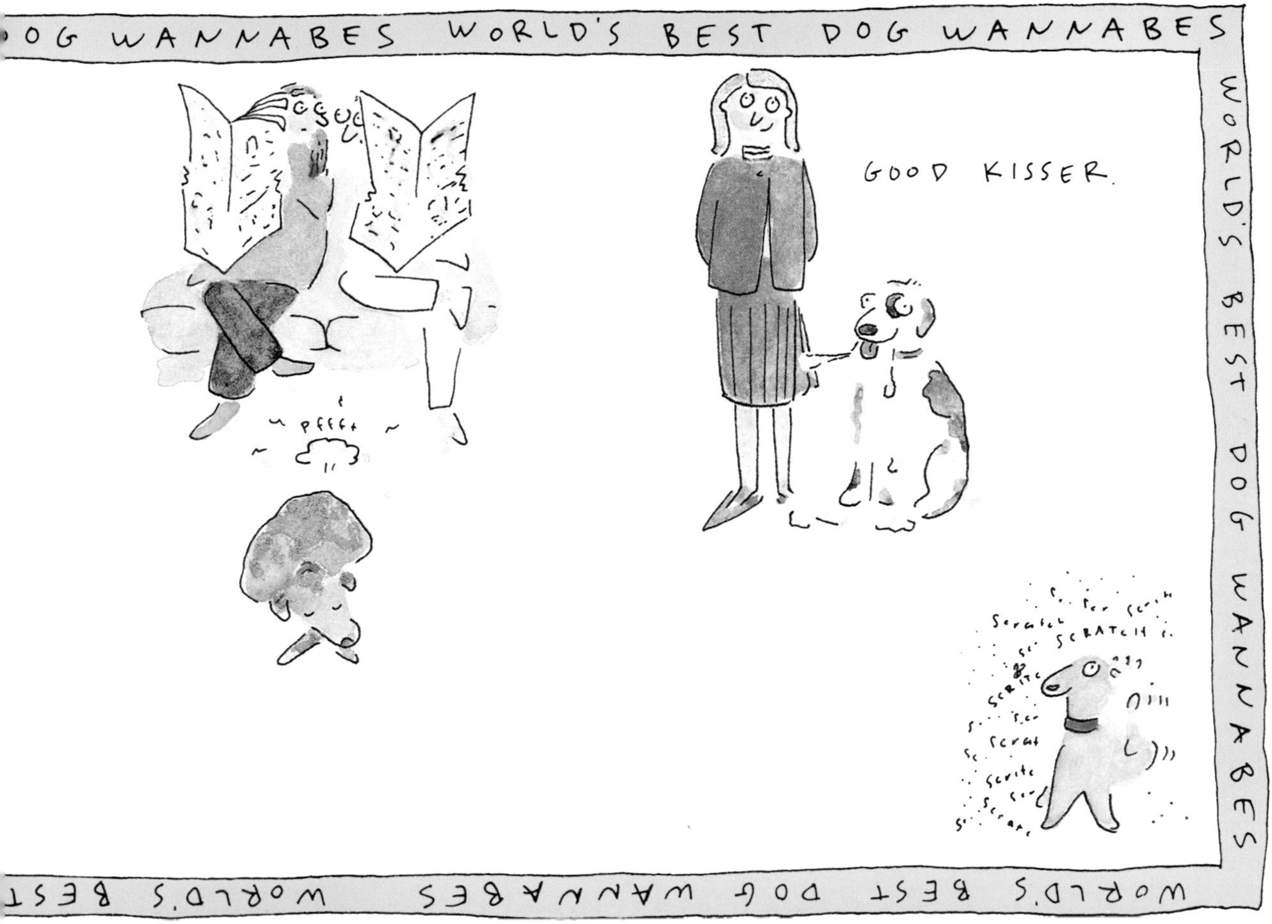
OG WANNABES WORLD'S BEST DOG WANNABES
WORLD'S BEST DOG WANNABES
WORLD'S BEST DOG WANNABES WORLD'S BEST
pffft
GOOD KISSER.
Scratch
SCRATCH

MY DOG LOVES MY CAT

THE MOMENT in MANTRAS

my Dog: oh please like me
oh please . . .

my Cat: Lord grant me
the serenity . . .

WHICH IS NOT TO SAY THE REVERSE IS TRUE

BUT THAT DOESN'T SEEM TO BOTHER HER MUCH.

Come to think of it —
nothing does.

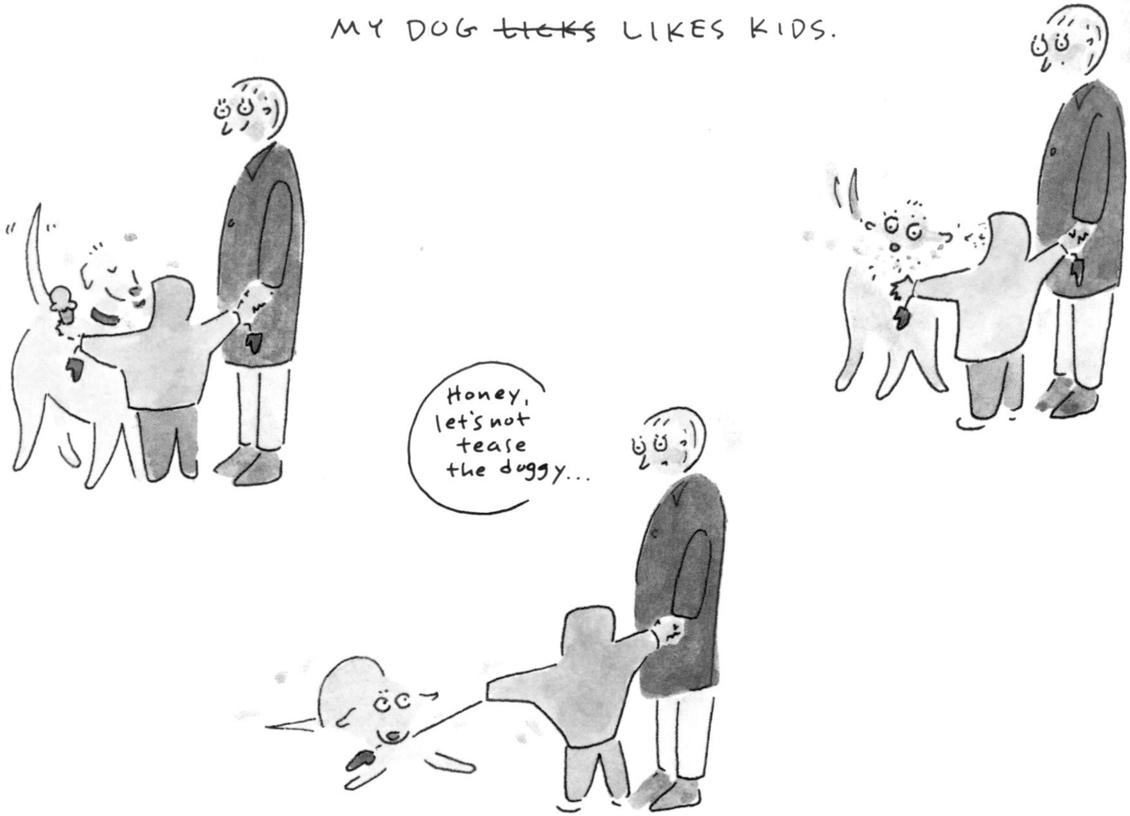
MY DOG ~~licks~~ LIKES KIDS.
Honey, let's not tease the doggy...

SHE DOESN'T HAVE A MEAN BONE IN HER BODY.

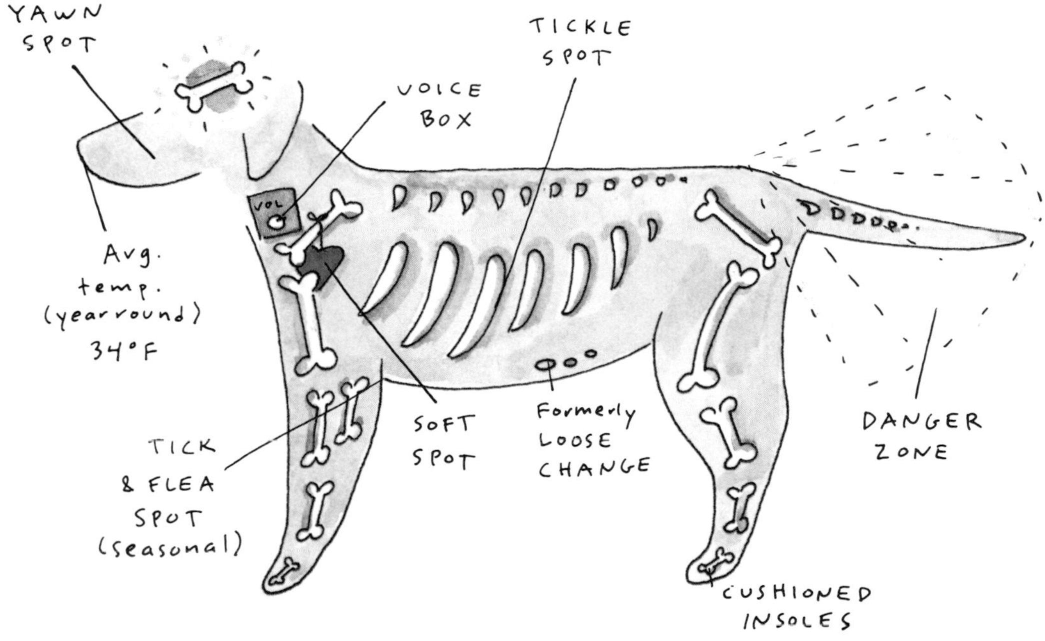
YAWN SPOT
VOL
Avg. temp. (yearround) 34°F
VOICE BOX
TICKLE SPOT
SOFT SPOT
Formerly LOOSE CHANGE
TICK & FLEA SPOT (seasonal)
DANGER ZONE
CUSHIONED INSOLES

MY DOG HAS THE WORLD'S SOFTEST EARS

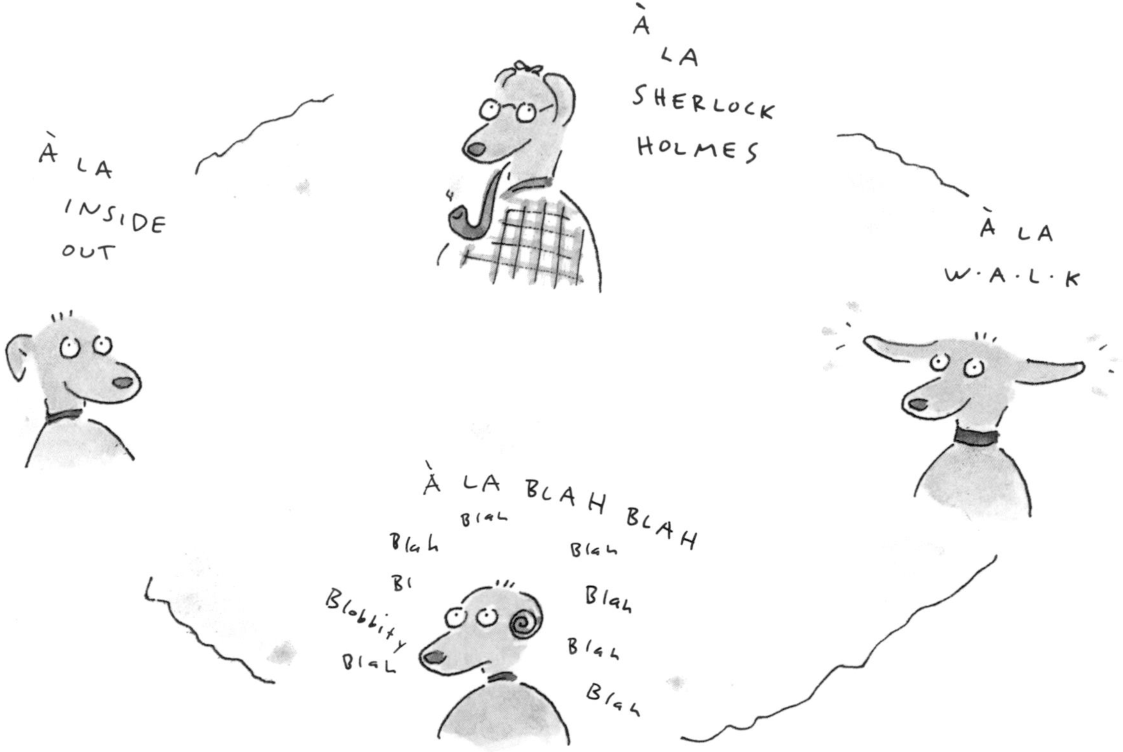
À LA SHERLOCK HOLMES
À LA INSIDE OUT
À LA W·A·L·K
À LA BLAH BLAH
Blah
Blah
Bl
Blobbity
Blah
Blah
Blah
Blah
Blah

AND VERY EXPRESSIVE EYES.

SHEEPISH
BORED
ALERT
MAD
SLEEPY
SNEAKY
COY
ANNOYED
SHINING

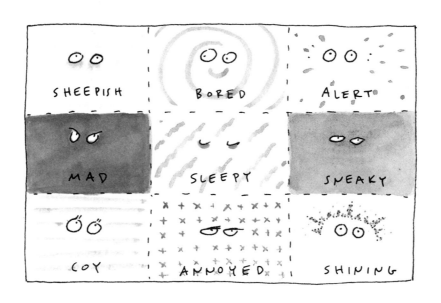

SHE CAN TELL WHEN I'M COMING

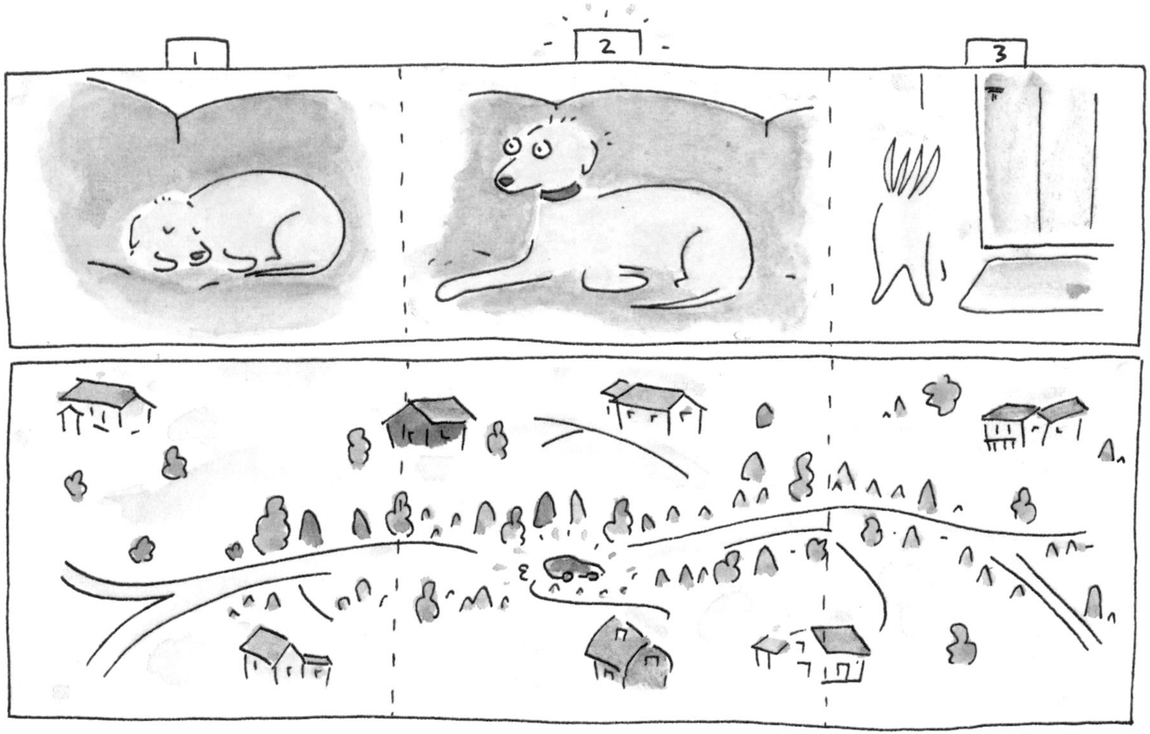
1
2
3

AND SHE GIVES THE BEST GREETINGS

even if you've only been gone 45 seconds.

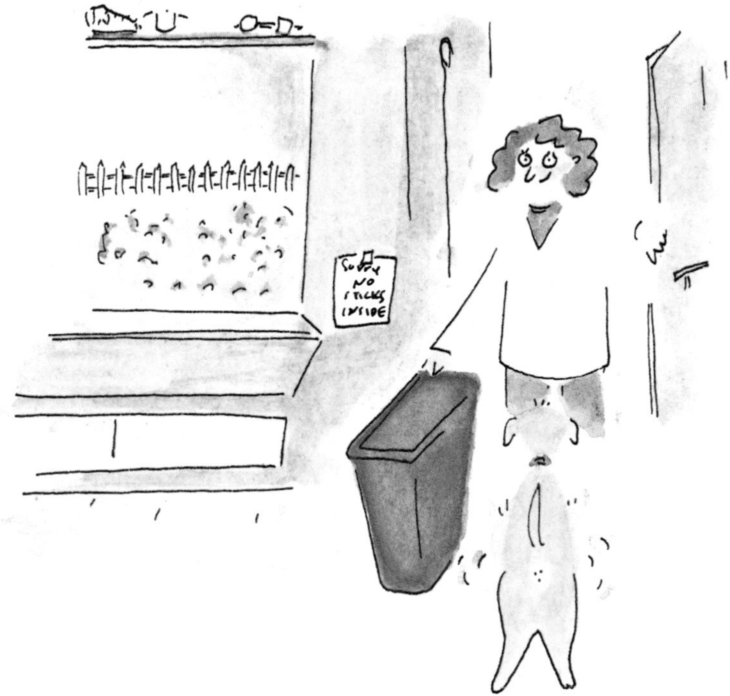
SORRY NO STICKS INSIDE

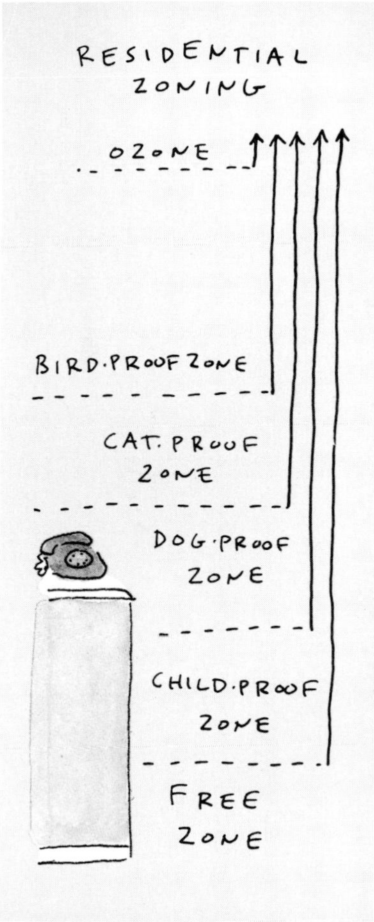
RESIDENTIAL ZONING
OZONE
BIRD·PROOF ZONE
CAT·PROOF ZONE
DOG·PROOF ZONE
CHILD·PROOF ZONE
FREE ZONE

MY DOG IS NO TROUBLE AT BEDTIME—
SAY THE WORDS AND SHE GOES RIGHT TO BED.

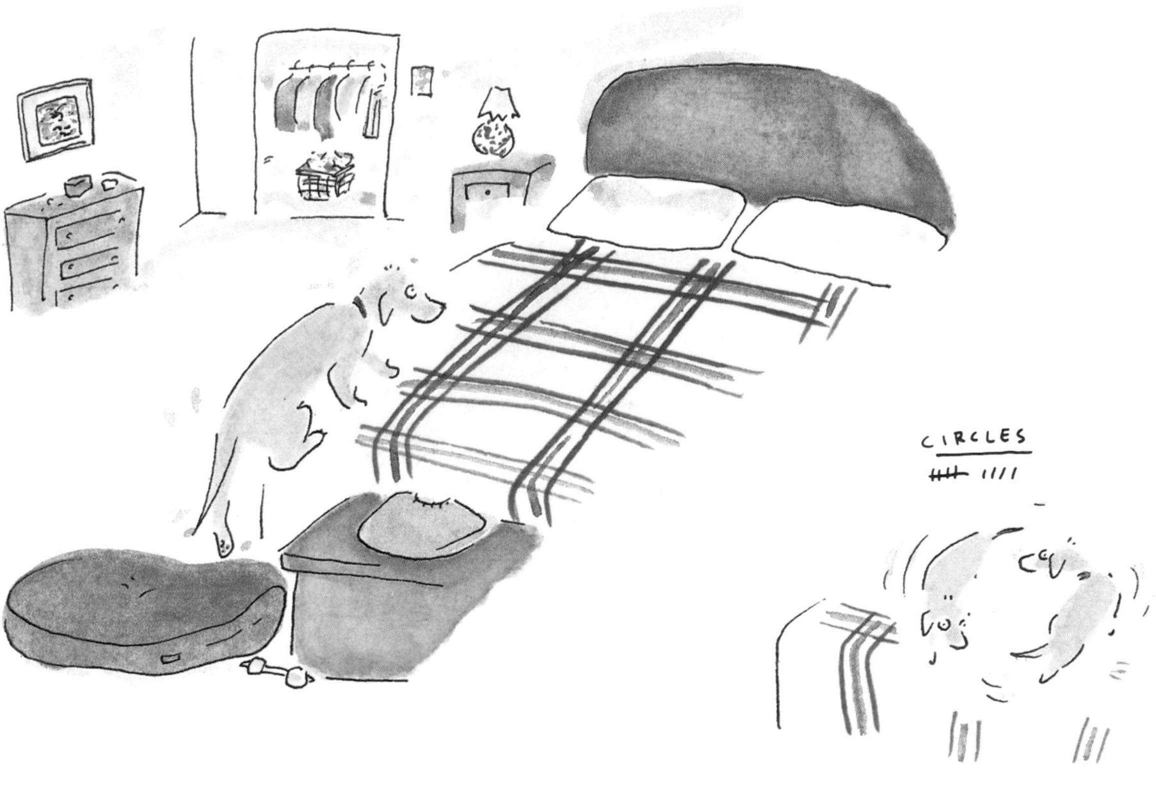
CIRCLES

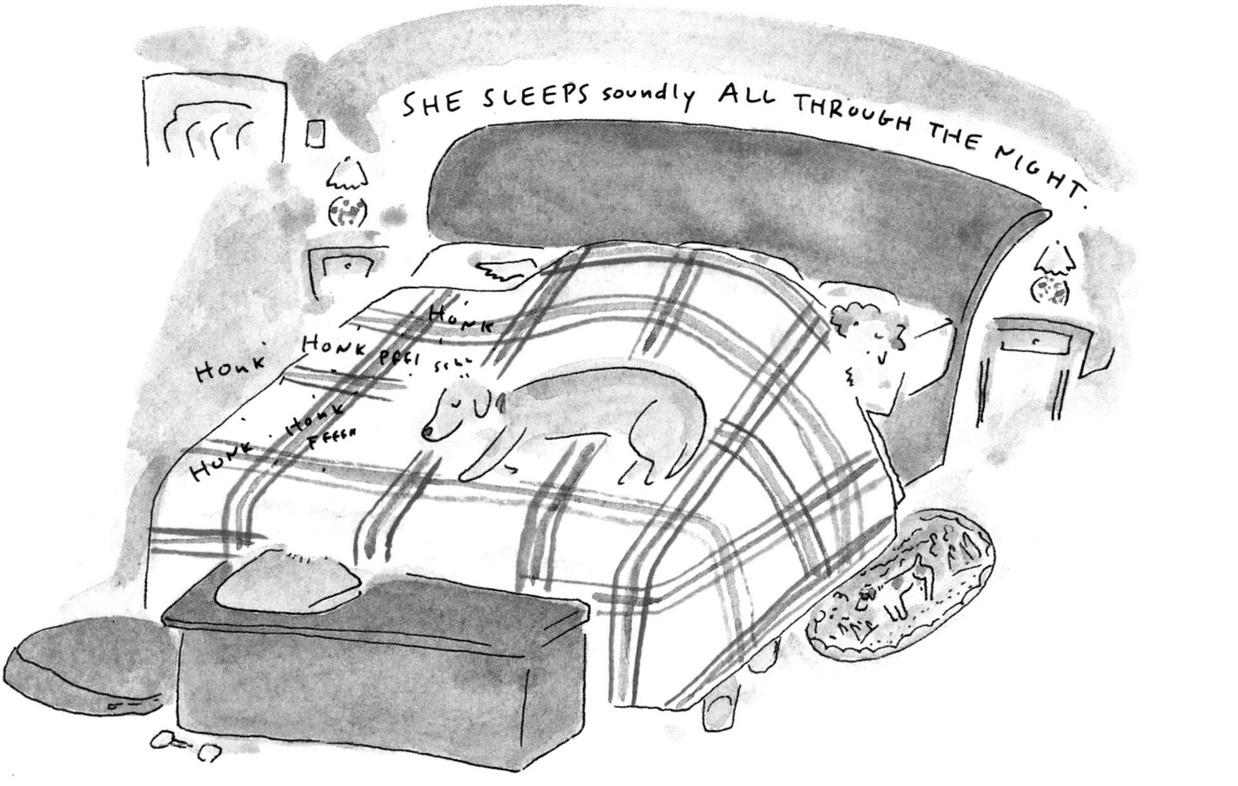
SHE SLEEPS soundly ALL THROUGH THE NIGHT.
HONK
HONK
HONK
HONK
HONK

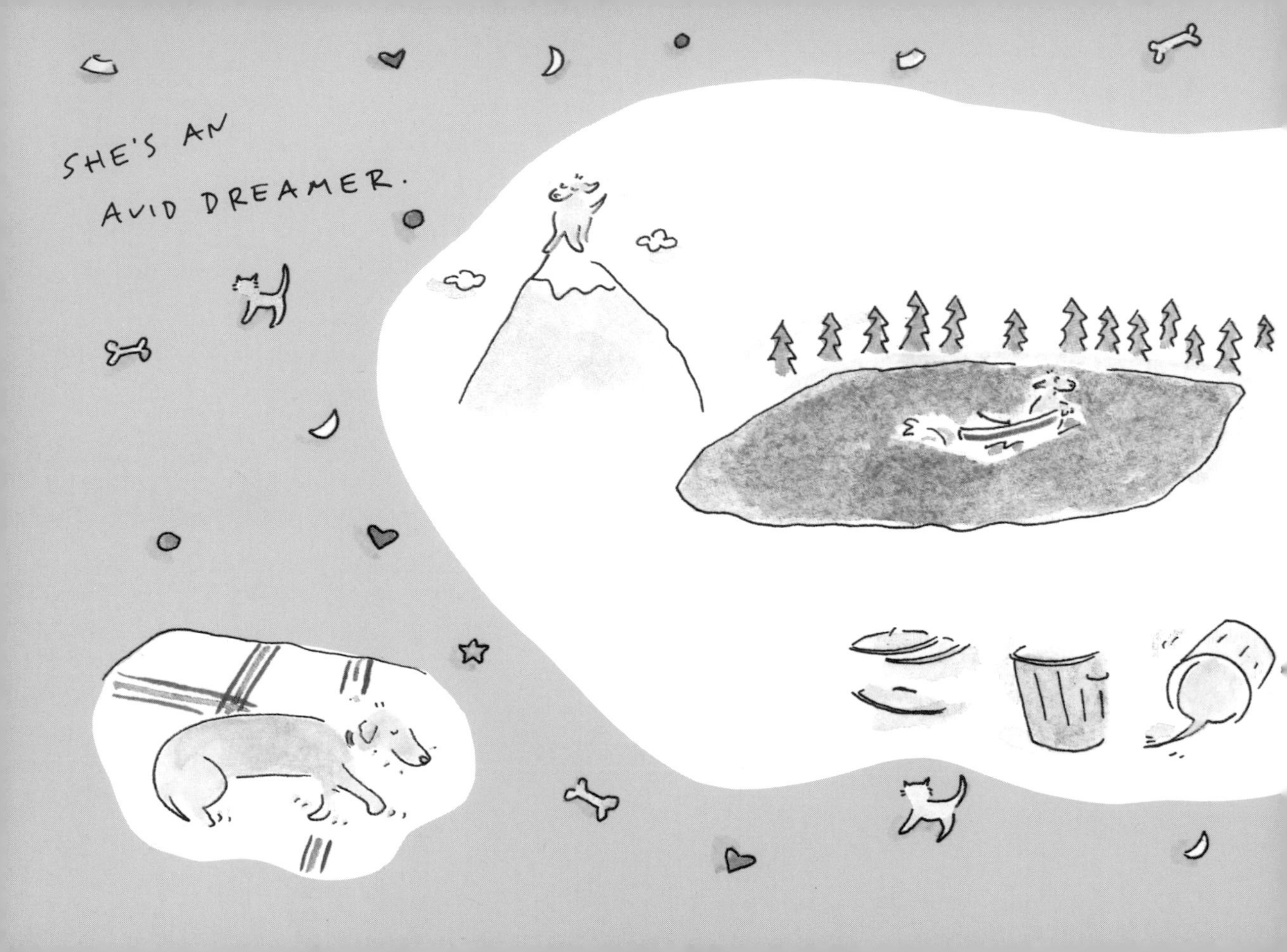
SHE'S AN AVID DREAMER.

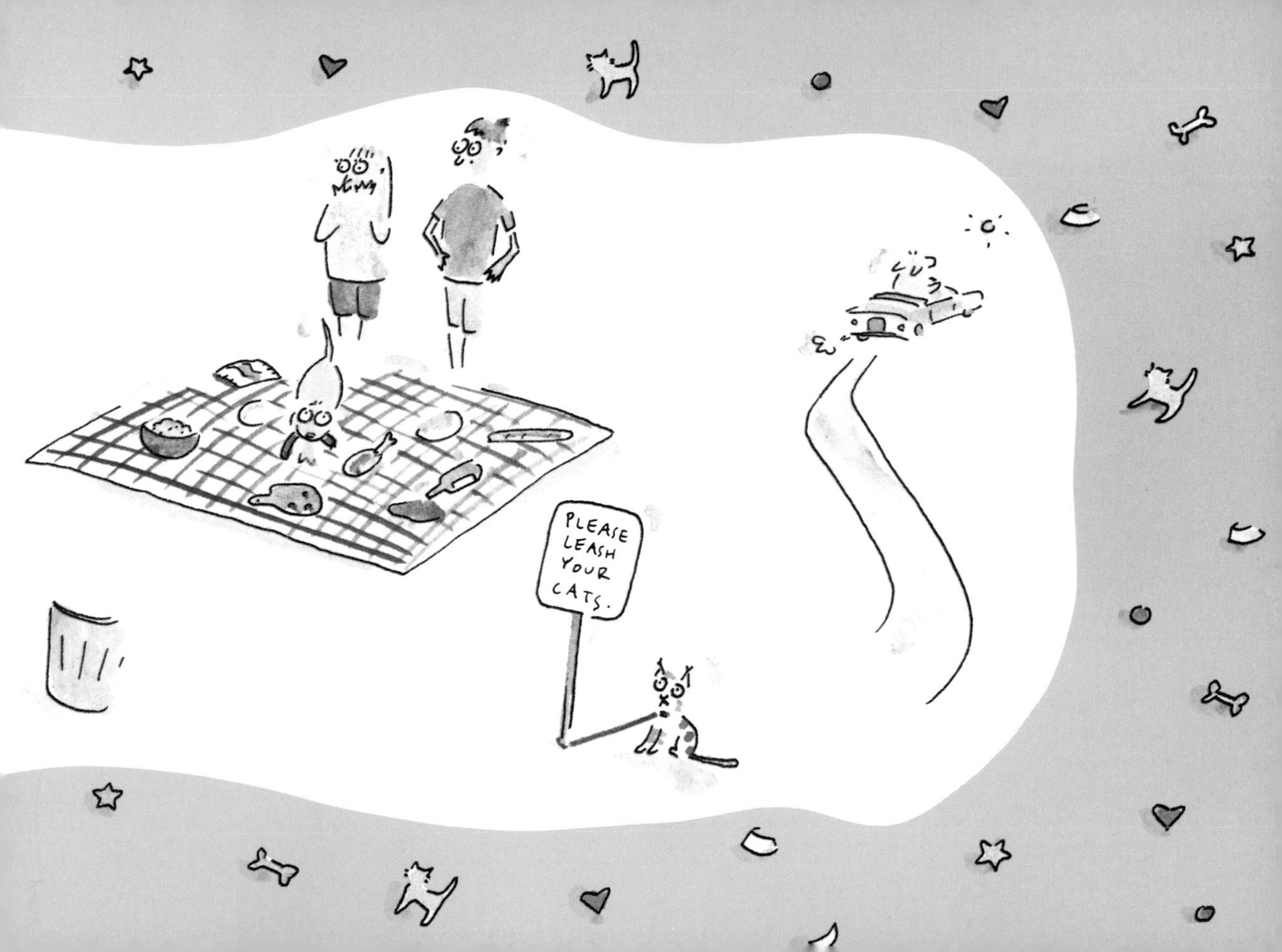
PLEASE LEASH YOUR CATS.

MY DOG'S A MORNING PERSON.

AFTER

A LITTLE

S-T-R-ETCHING...

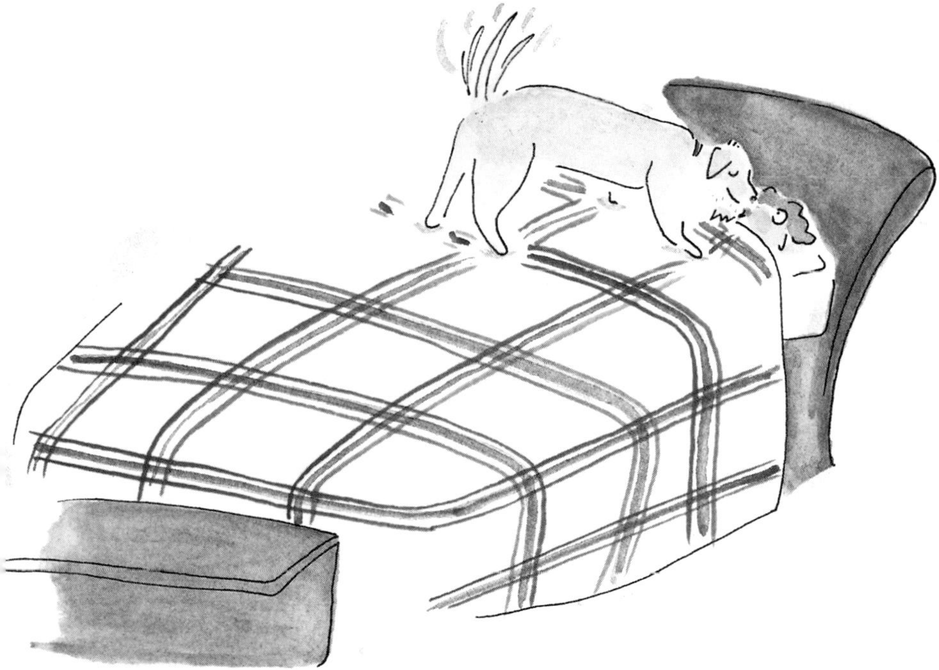

SHE'S UP'N'WAGGING.

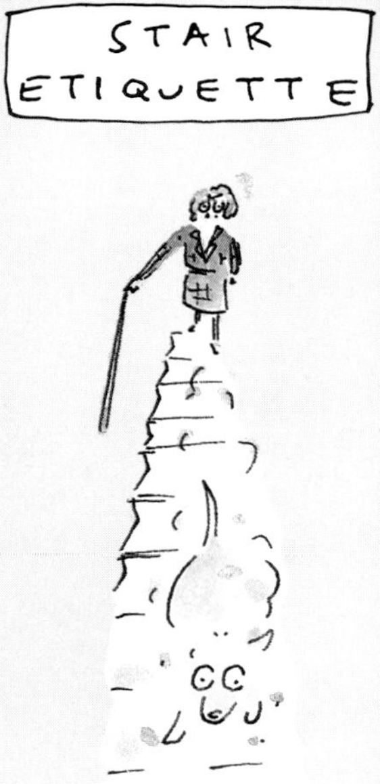
STAIR ETIQUETTE

DOGS before AGE before BEAUTY.

PEOPLE SAY THAT DOGS REFLECT THEIR OWNERS.

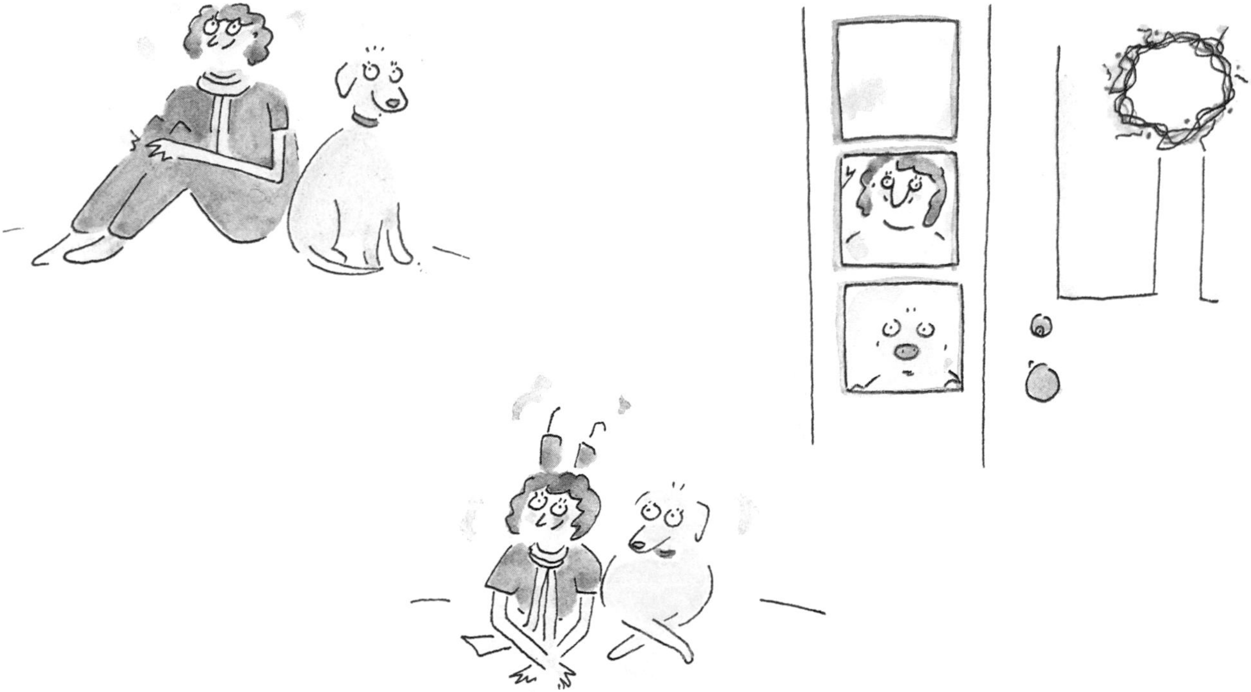

SHE'S MUCH MORE EVEN-TEMPERED.

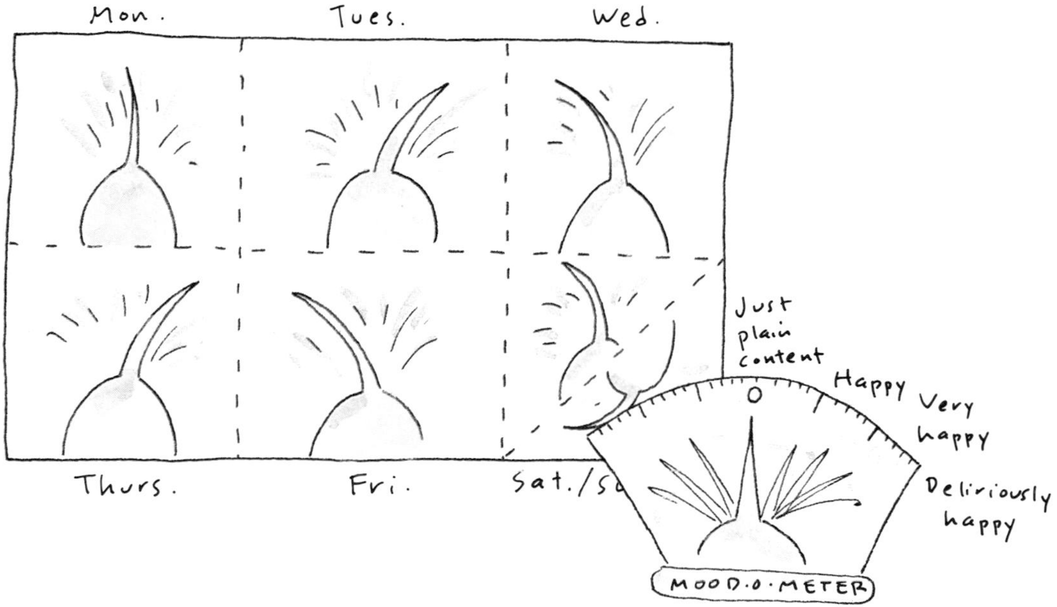
Mon.
Tues.
Wed.
Thurs.
Fri.
Sat./
Just plain content
Happy
Very happy
Deliriously happy
0
MOOD-O-METER

NEGATIVE POSITIVE CORRELATION

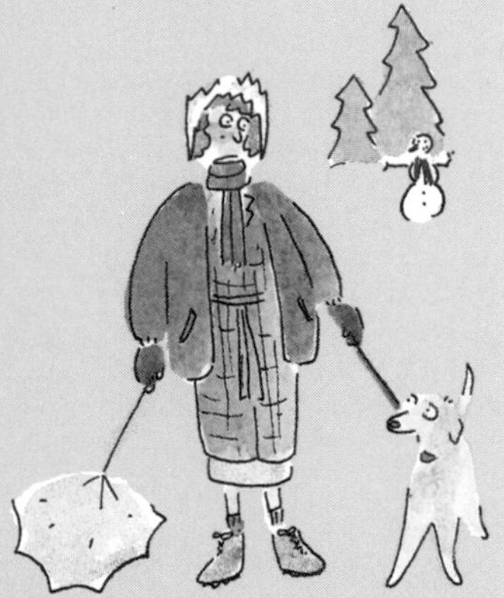

THE WORSE THE WEATHER THE LONGER IT TAKES TO FIND A PLACE TO GO TO THE BATHROOM.

MY DOG COMES WHEN YOU CALL HER.

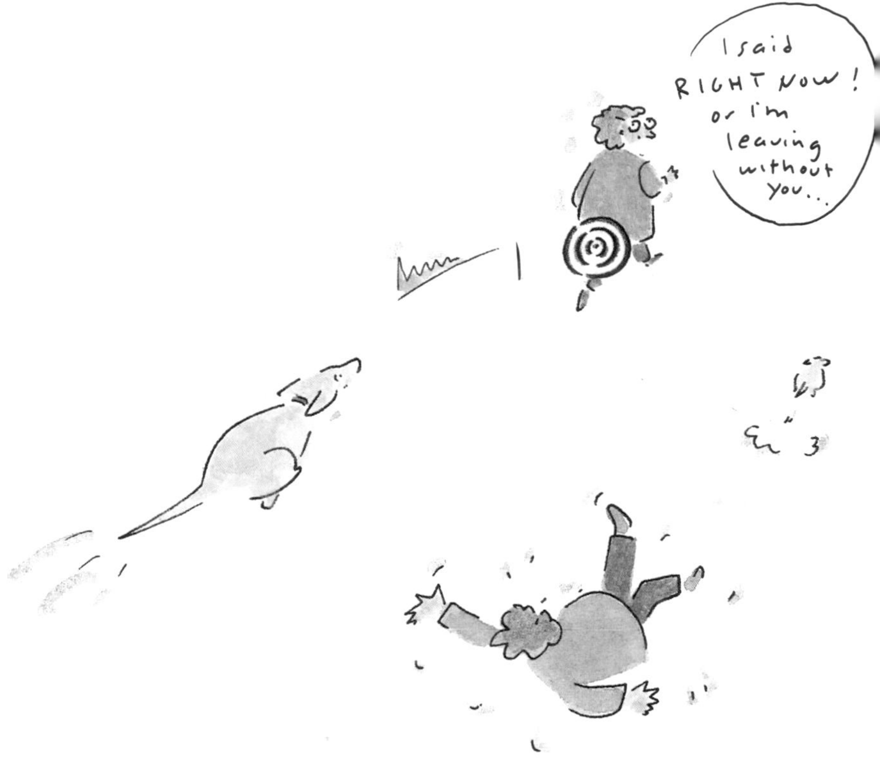
I said RIGHT NOW! or I'm leaving without you...

IN FACT, I'D NEVER HAVE TO KEEP HER ON A LEASH

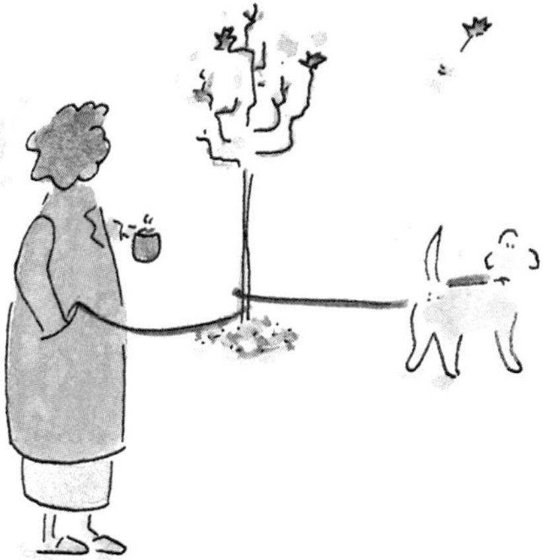

if it weren't for the cars, cats, dogs, squirrels, leaves, low-flying planes, bikes . . .

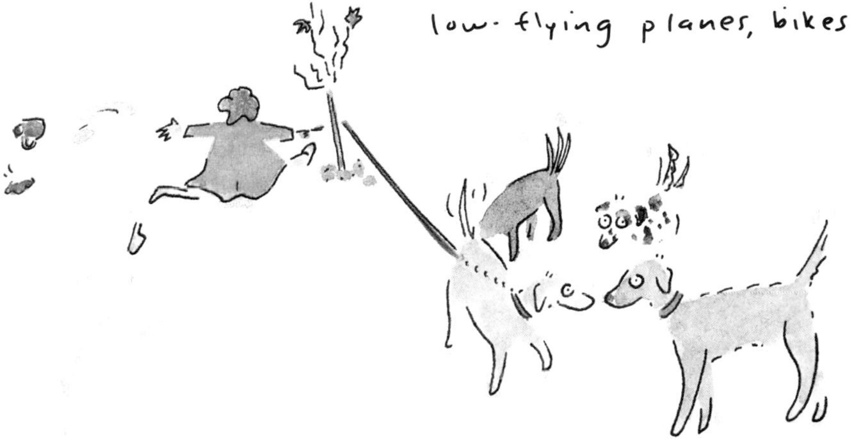

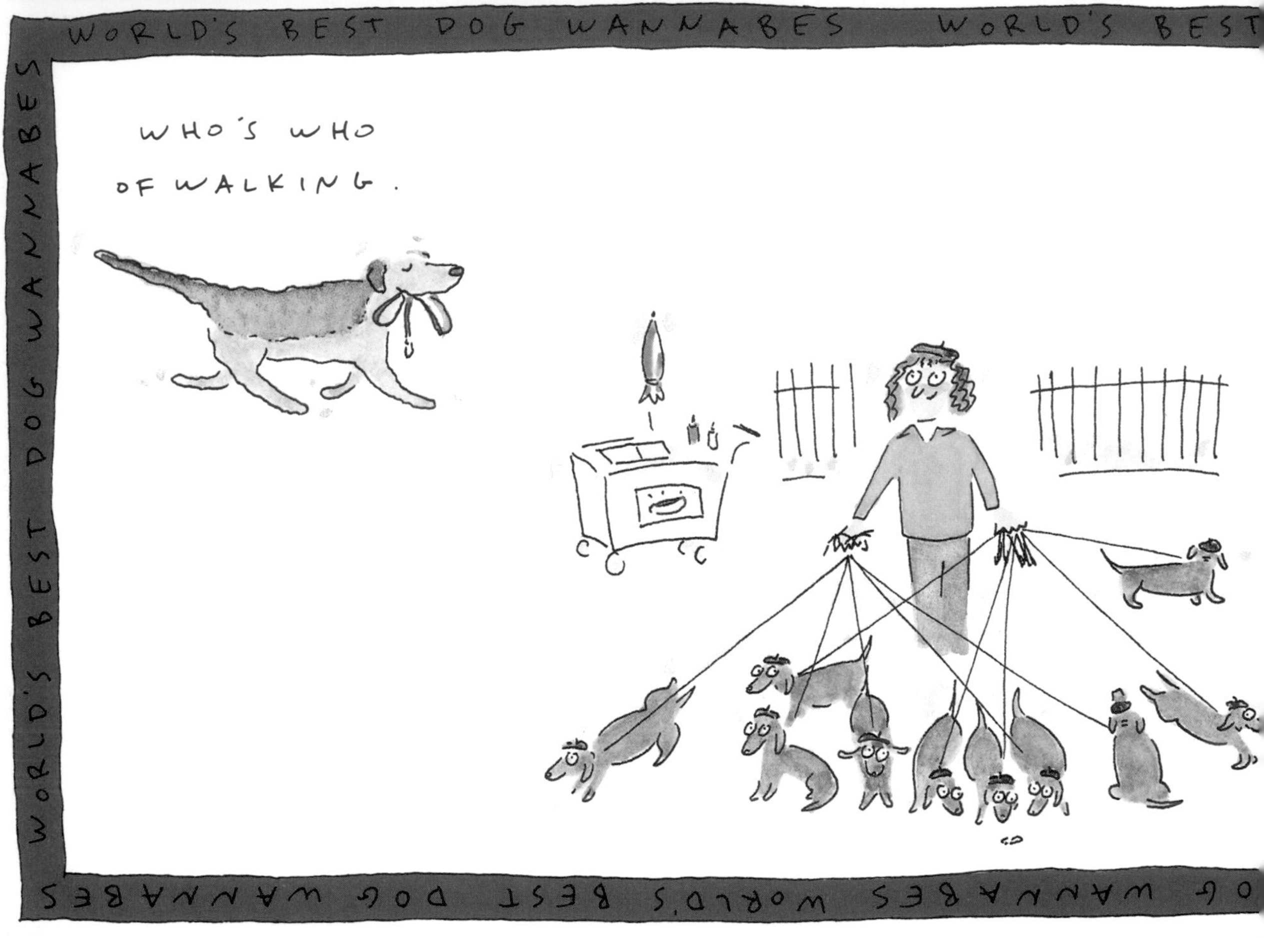
WORLD'S BEST DOG WANNABES
WHO'S WHO OF WALKING.

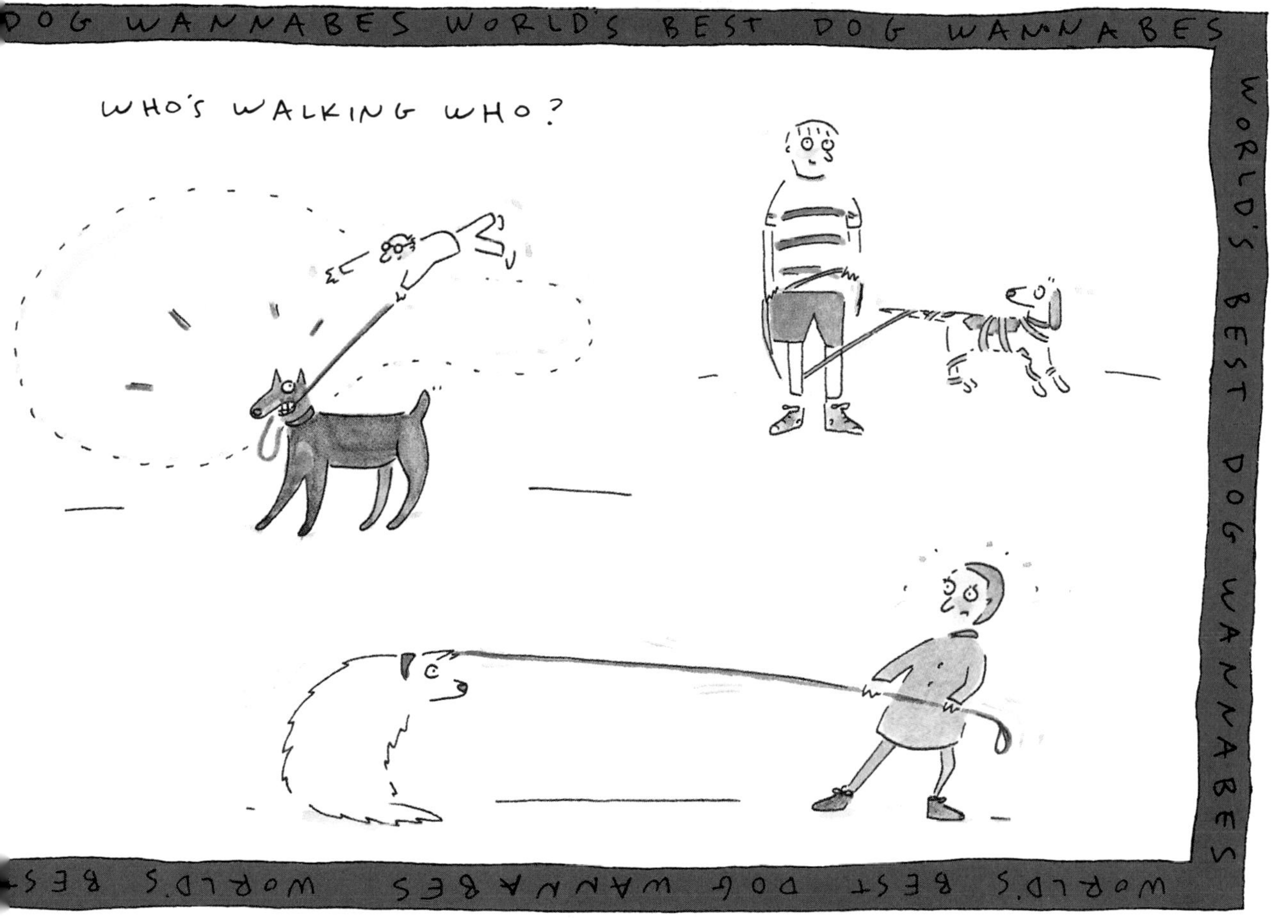
DOG WANNABES WORLD'S BEST DOG WANNABES
WORLD'S BEST DOG WANNABES
WORLD'S BEST DOG WANNABES WORLD'S BEST
WHO'S WALKING WHO?

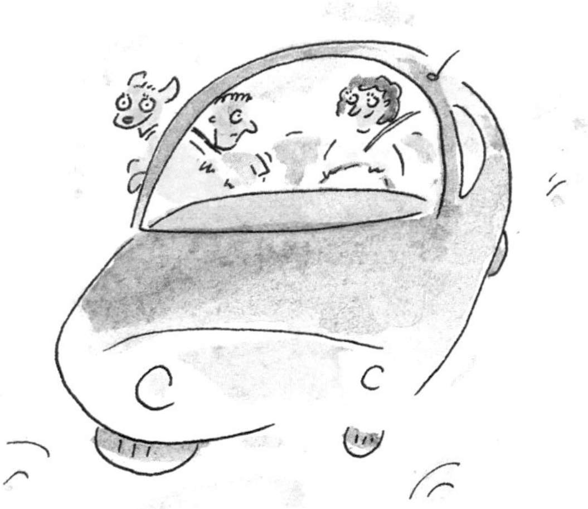

My dog is my co-pilot.

WAITING

1 (MISSISSIPPI)

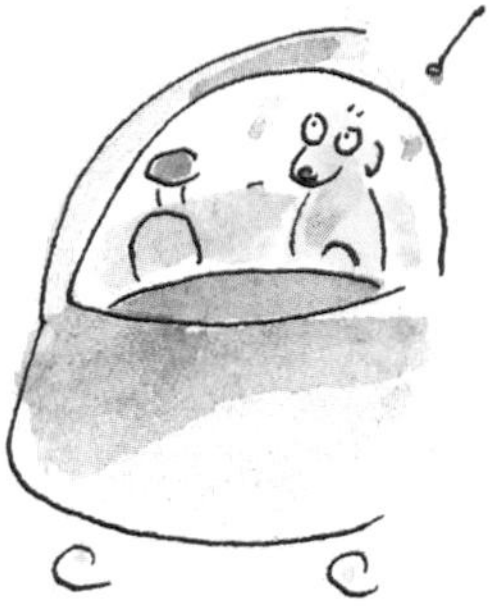

2 (MISSISSIPPI)

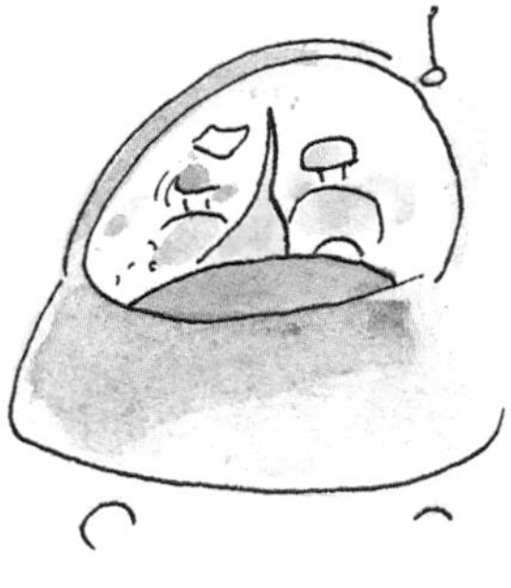

SHE ALWAYS KNOWS EXACTLY WHERE WE'RE GOING WAY BEFORE WE GET THERE.

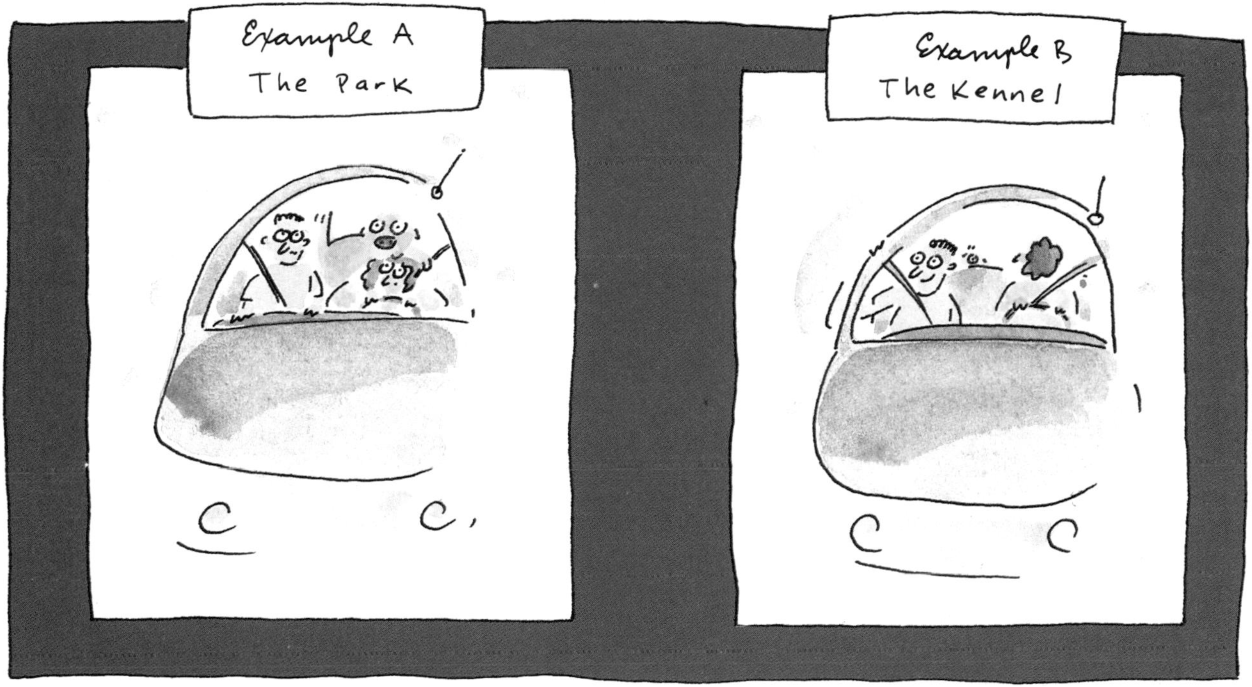
Example A
The Park
Example B
The Kennel

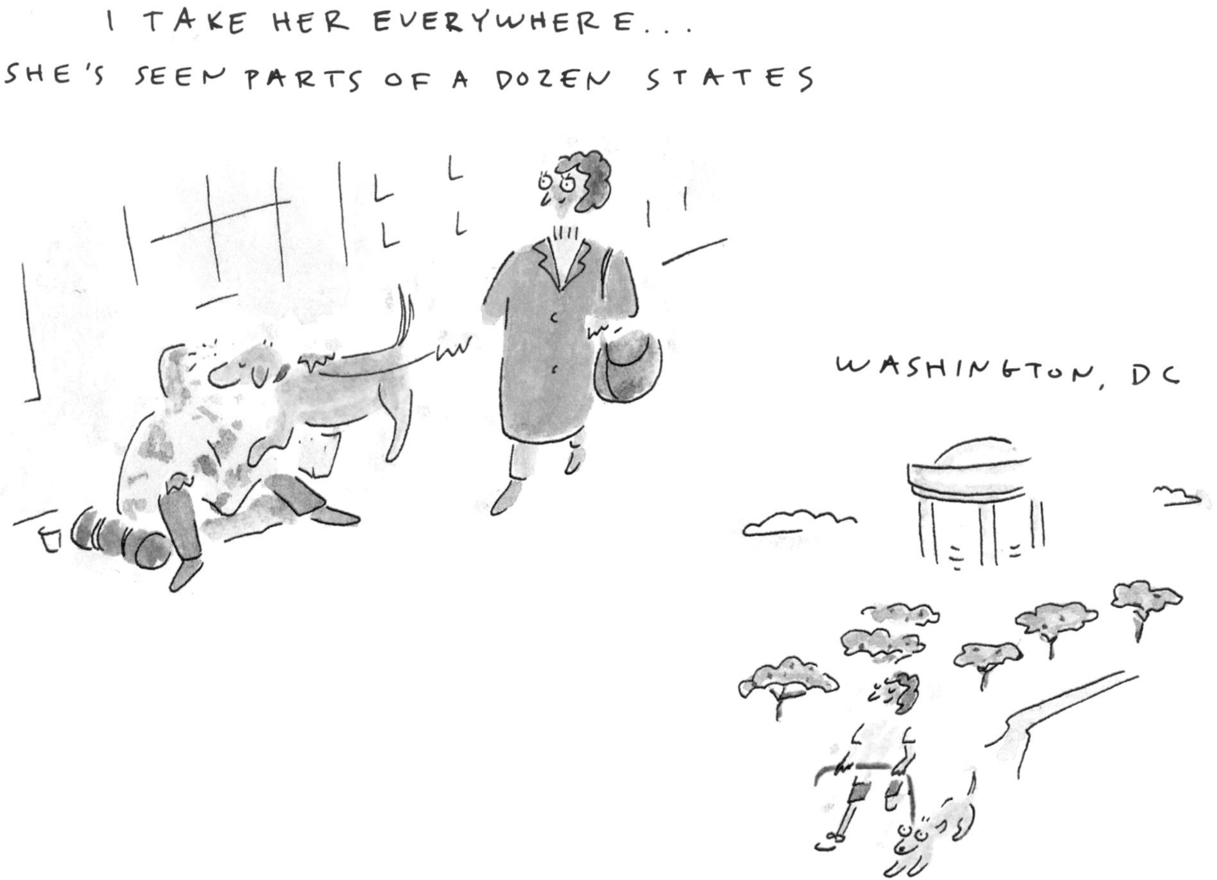
I TAKE HER EVERYWHERE...
SHE'S SEEN PARTS OF A DOZEN STATES
WASHINGTON, DC

AND CANADA.

EXPRESS

CHECK·IN

ELK·IN

: ELK·IN

INNKEEPER: Your dog does <u>not</u> go on the furniture, does he?

ME: On the furniture?

INNKPR: Good.

SHE MAY not BE THE WORLD'S BEST GUEST . . .

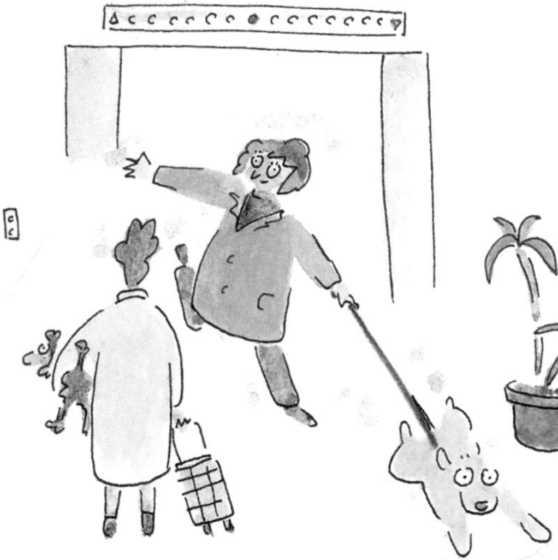

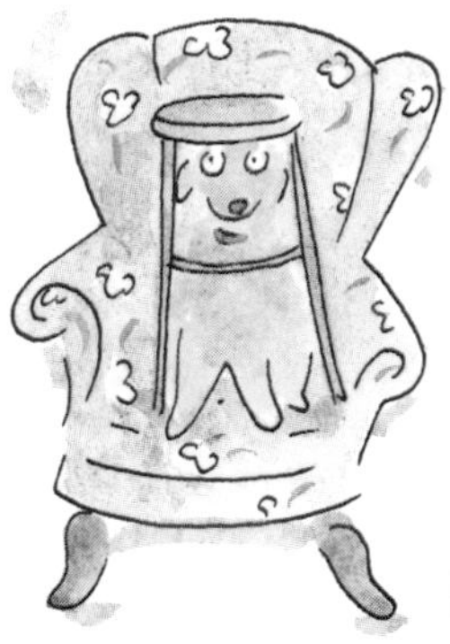

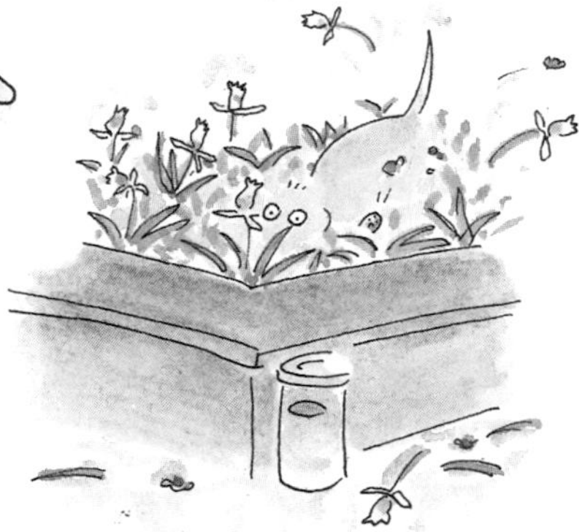

note: SOME PEOPLE PUT FURNITURE ON THEIR FURNITURE TO KEEP THEIR PETS OFF. THEIR FURNITURE.

She's the World's Best Dog.

THE HOUSE RULES (Pick one)

KEEP THE DOG OUTSIDE

or

LET THE DOG INSIDE but
NOT IN EVERY ROOM

or

LET THE DOG IN EVERY ROOM
BUT NOT ON ANY FURNITURE

or

LET THE DOG ON THE OLD
FURNITURE

or

LET THE DOG ON ANY OLE
FURNITURE

or

LET THE DOG ON THE BED
by invitation only

or

LET THE DOG UNDER THE
COVERS

a.k.a. (THE DOG LETS YOU
ON THE BED by
invitation only..)

THE DOG RULES

MY DOG IS BRAVE.

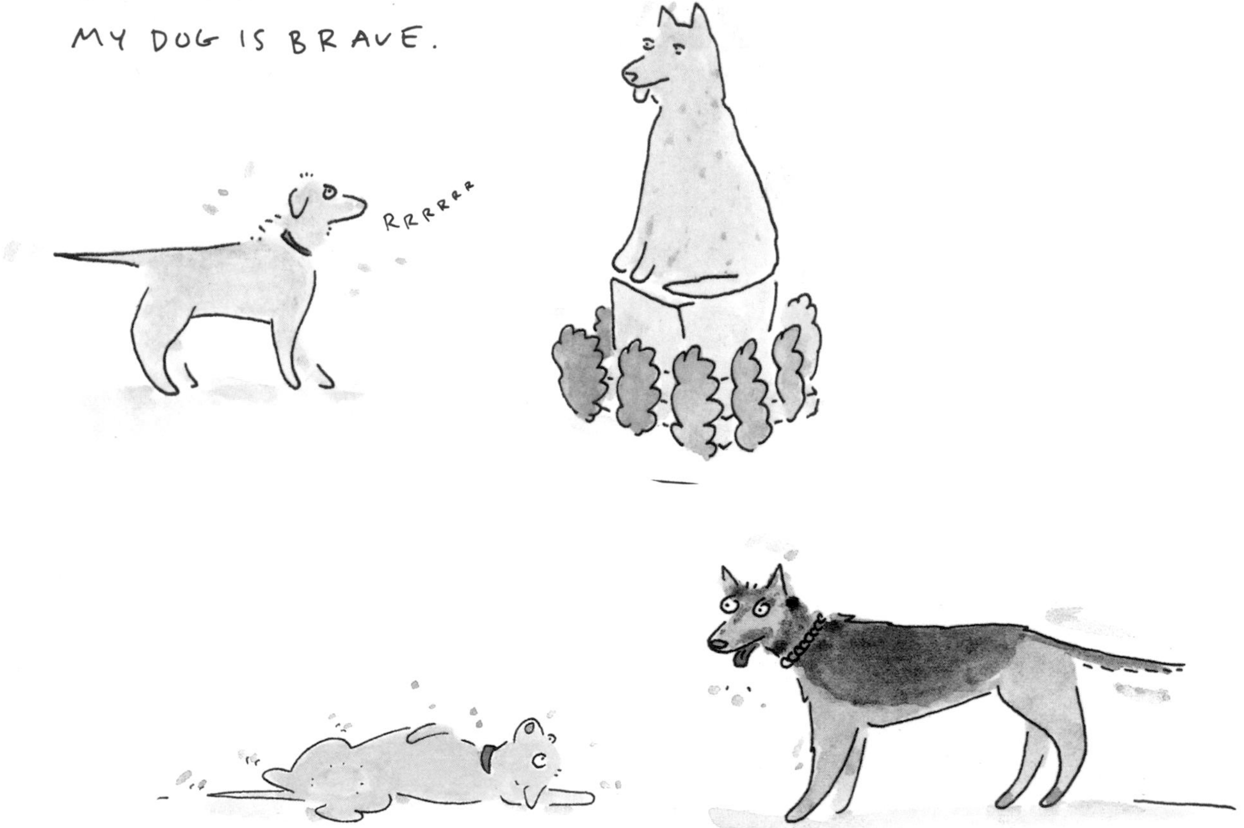
RRRRRR

She's not stupid.

SHE HAS A HEALTHY RESPECT FOR MEDICINE.

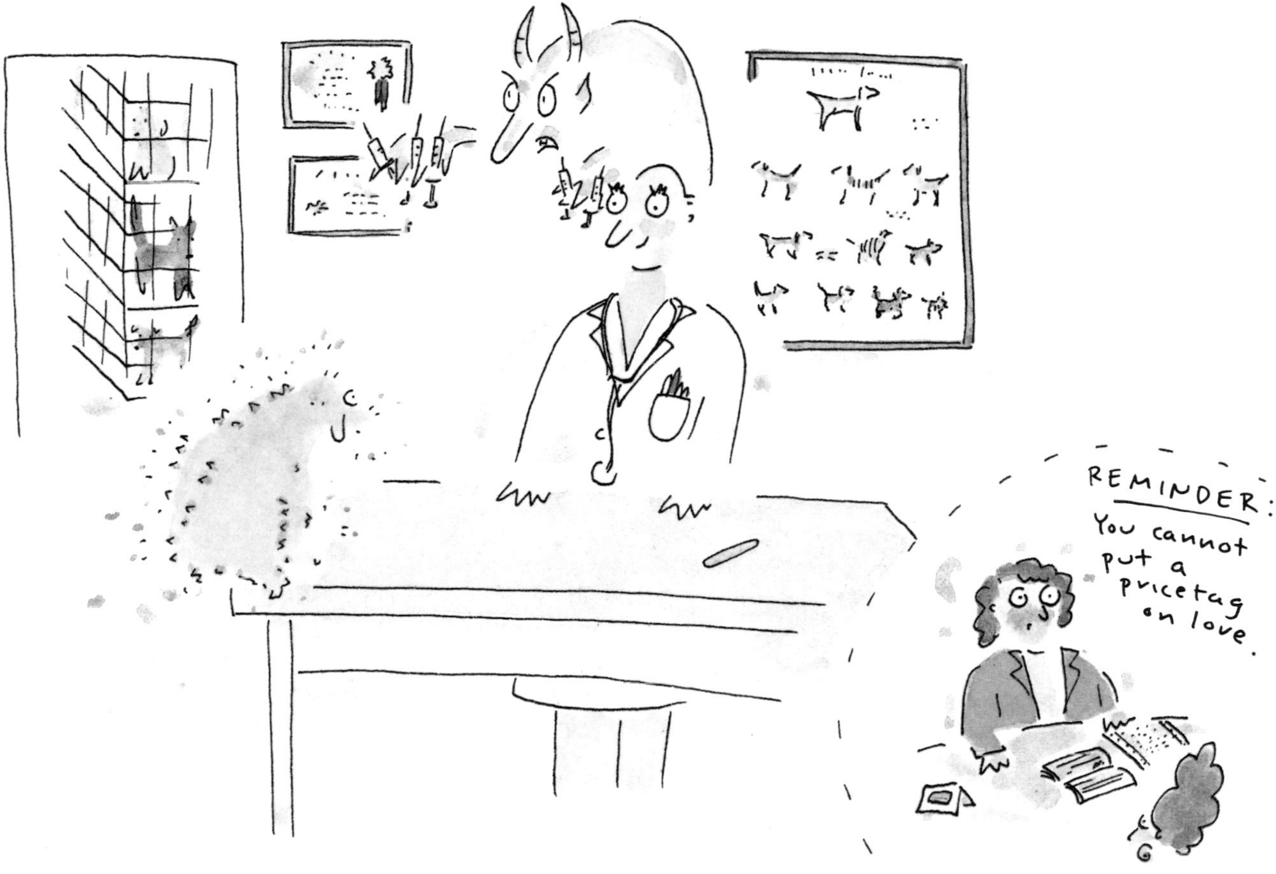
REMINDER: You cannot put a pricetag on love.

ETYMOLOGY
of a NAME
_____

My dog's WYLIE

SMILEY

BOO BOO (PILEY)

WYLIE BONES

MRS. Y. LEE BONES

MRS. BONES

MRS. B. or just plain
MRS.

MRS. B. OOGERSHNAM

BOOGIE for short

BROWNIE

MRS. BROWN

PROFESSOR BROWN

MY DOG SWALLOWS PILLS.

SHE LOVES PRAISE or anything that sounds like praise.

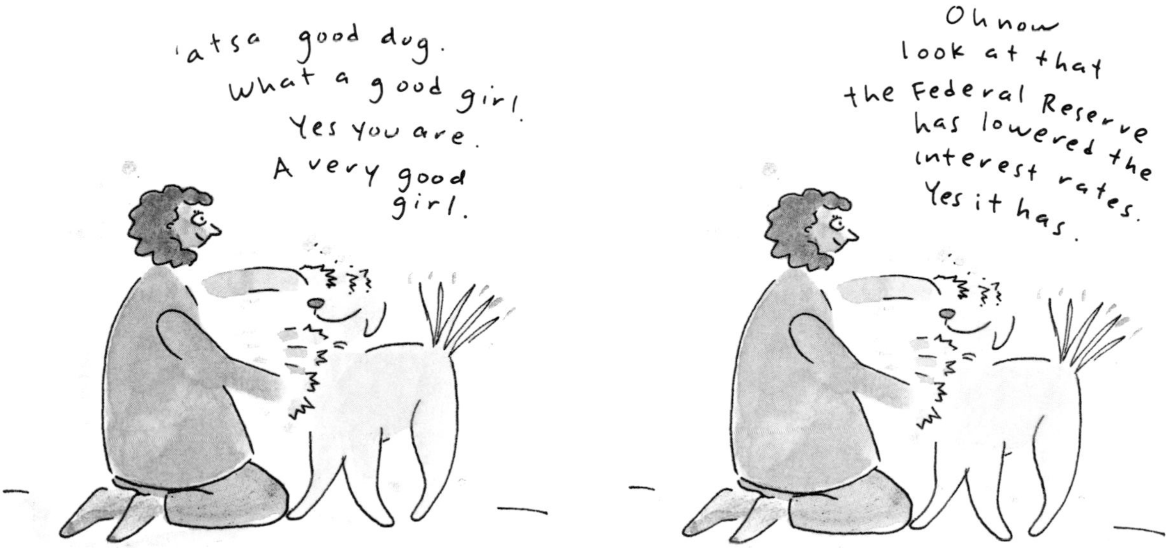
'atsa good dog. What a good girl. Yes you are. A very good girl.
Oh now look at that the Federal Reserve has lowered the interest rates. Yes it has.

SHE'S VERY FOND OF TREATS . . .

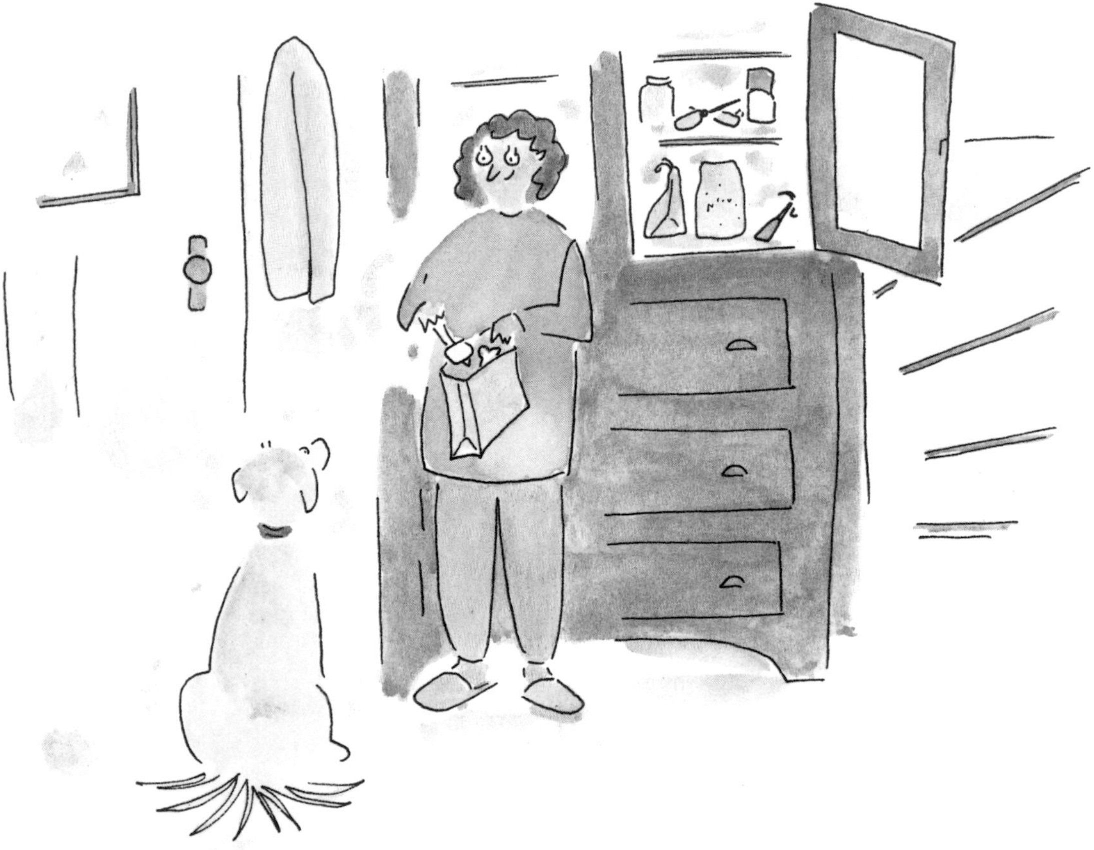

or anything that looks like treats.

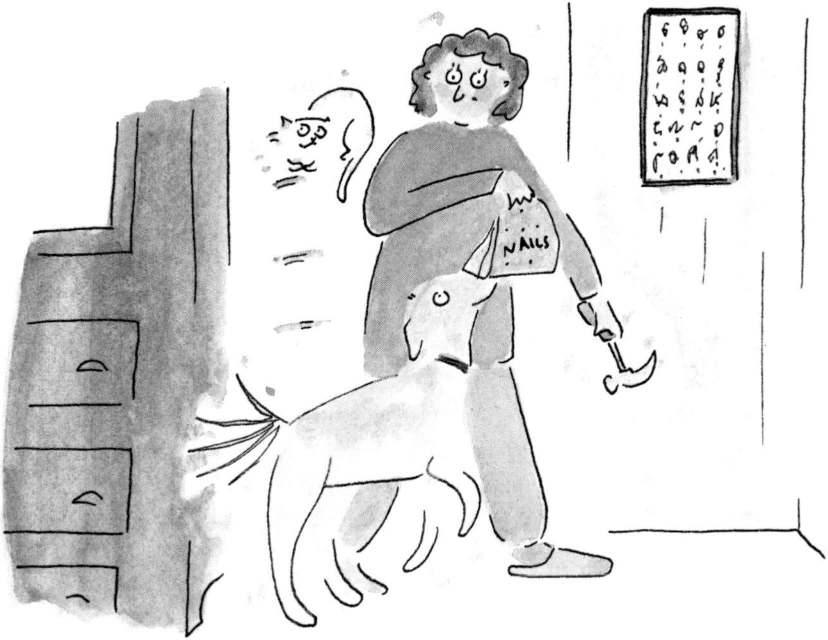
NAILS

MY DOG'S A REAL SHOWDOG. SHE DOES TRICKS...

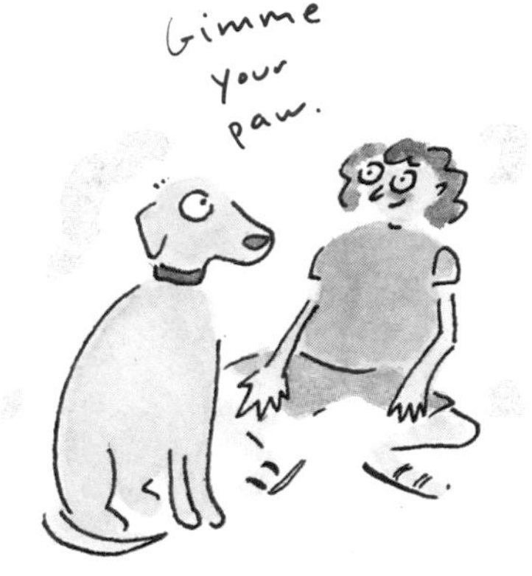
Gimme your paw.

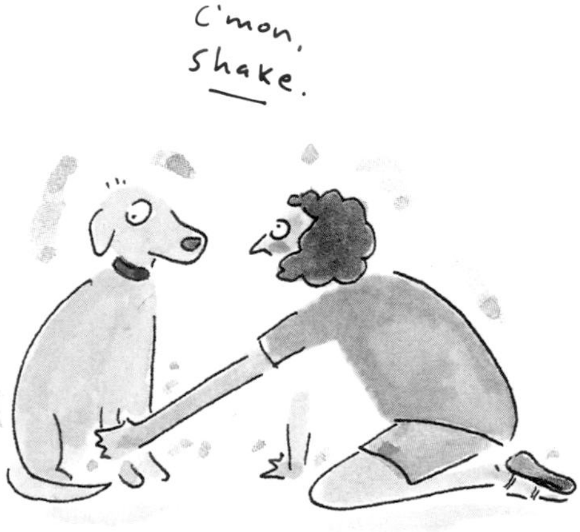
C'mon, shake.

SHAKE!

and IMPRESSIONS.

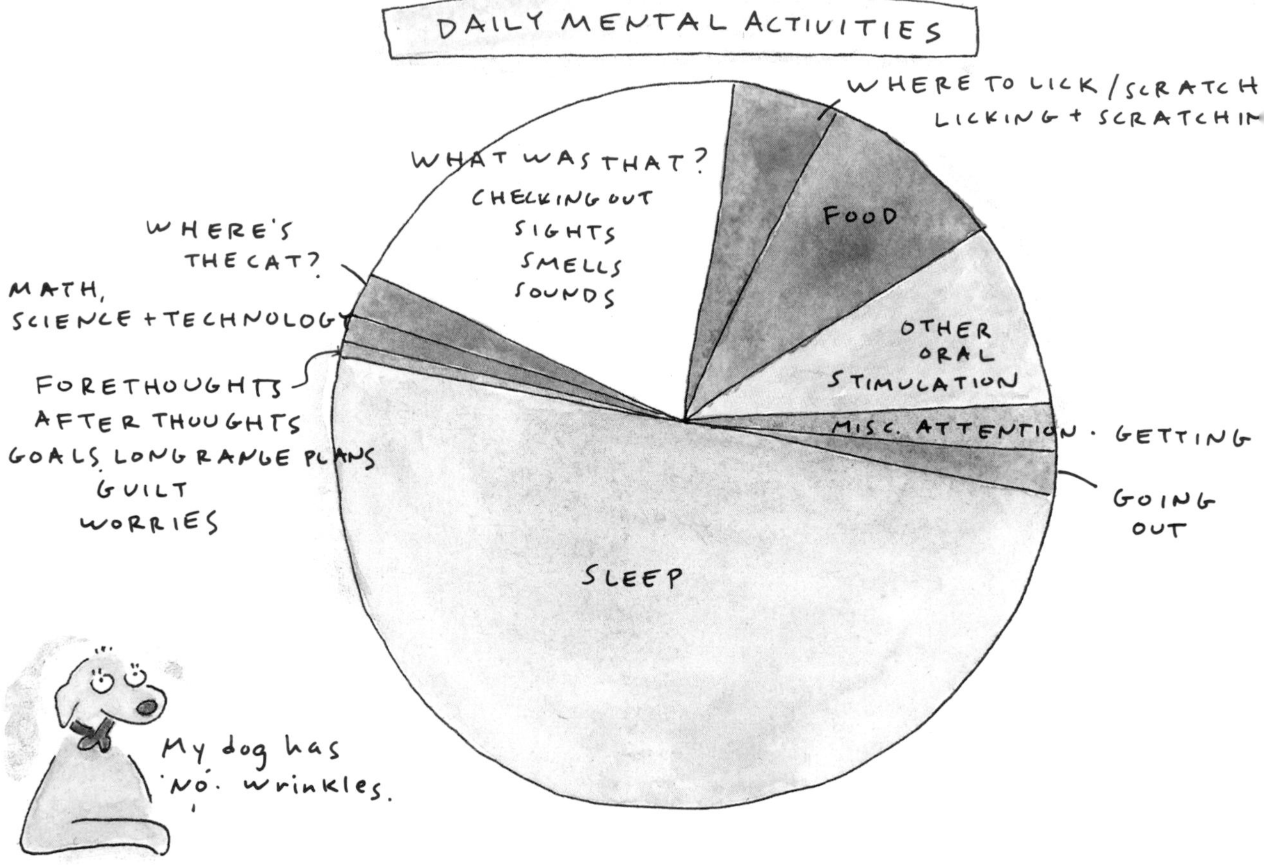
DAILY MENTAL ACTIVITIES
WHERE TO LICK / SCRATCH
LICKING + SCRATCHIN
WHAT WAS THAT?
CHECKING OUT
SIGHTS
SMELLS
SOUNDS
FOOD
OTHER
ORAL
STIMULATION
WHERE'S
THE CAT?
MATH,
SCIENCE + TECHNOLOGY
FORETHOUGHTS
AFTER THOUGHTS
GOALS, LONG RANGE PLANS
GUILT
WORRIES
MISC. ATTENTION · GETTING
GOING
OUT
SLEEP
My dog has
NO wrinkles.

MY DOG LOVES TO PLAY

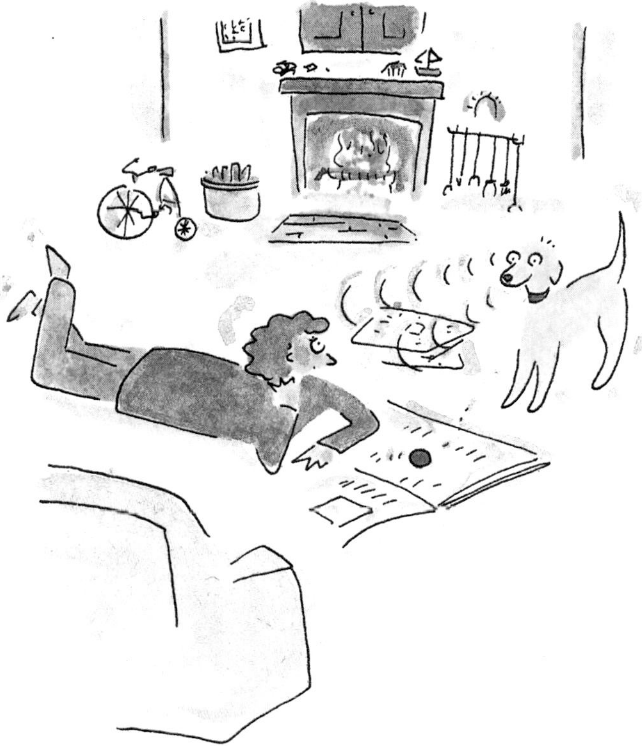

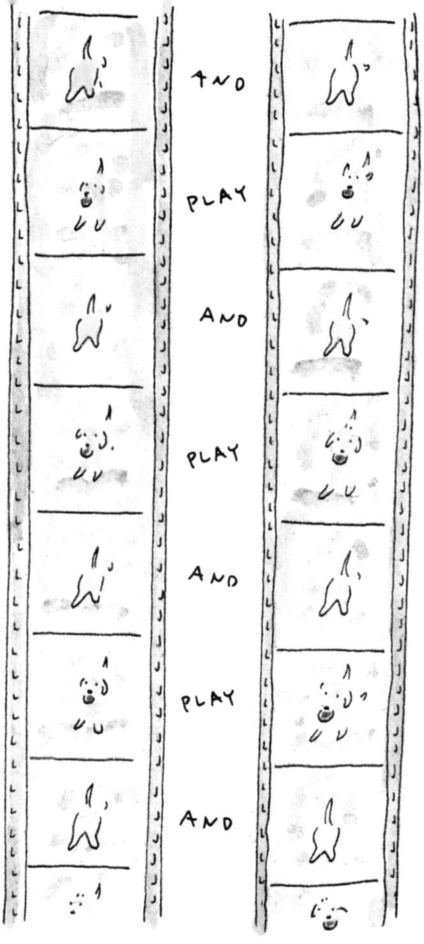
AND
PLAY
AND
PLAY
AND
PLAY
AND

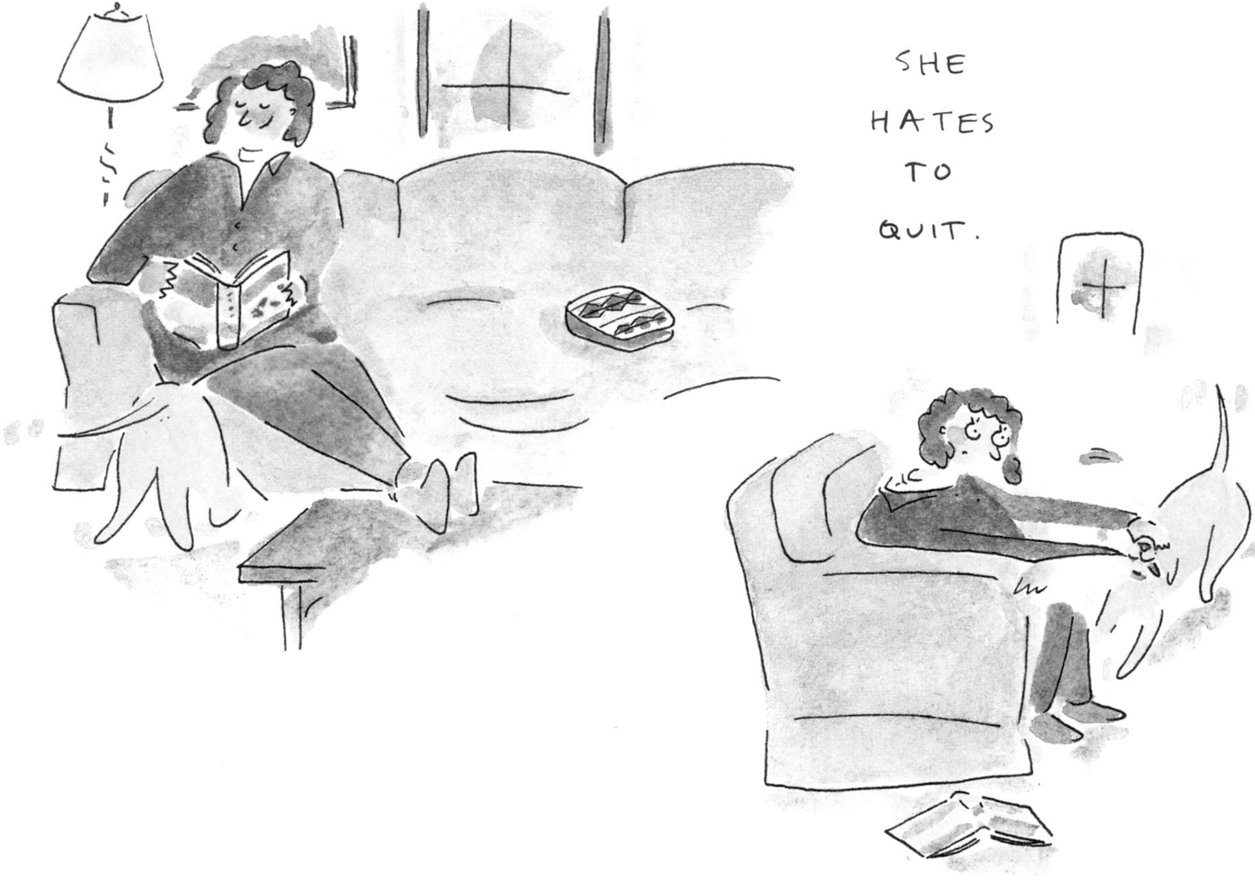
SHE HATES TO QUIT.

SHE definitely MAKES CLEANING UP MORE INTERESTING.

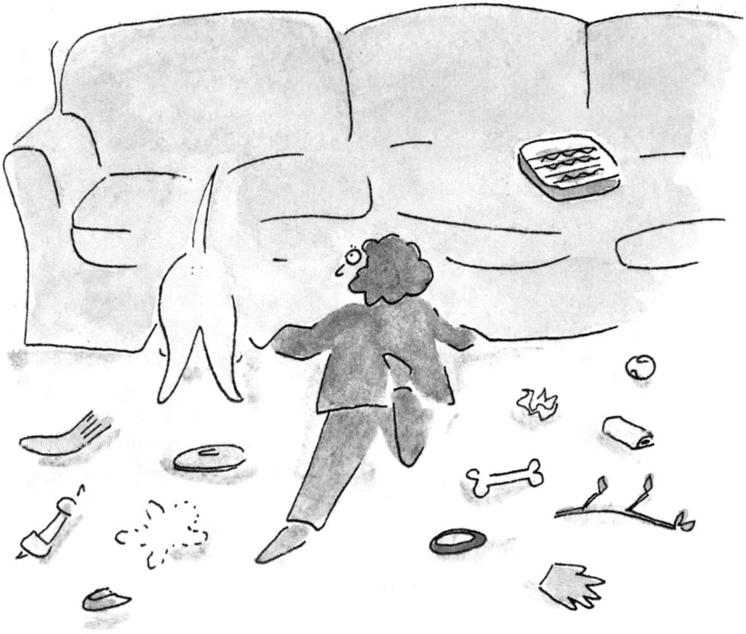

HOOVER VOODOO
The Vacuum Ritual

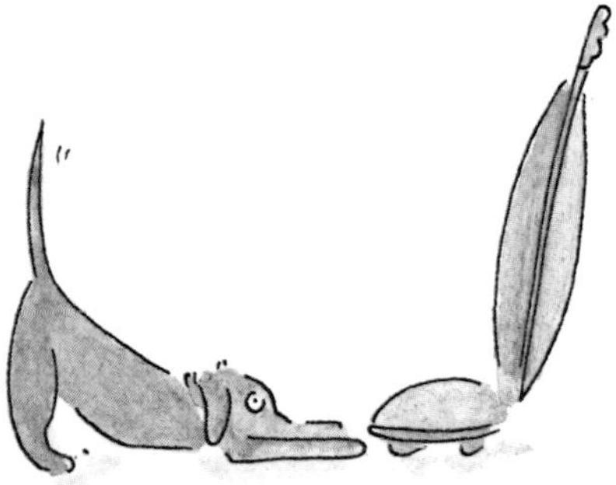

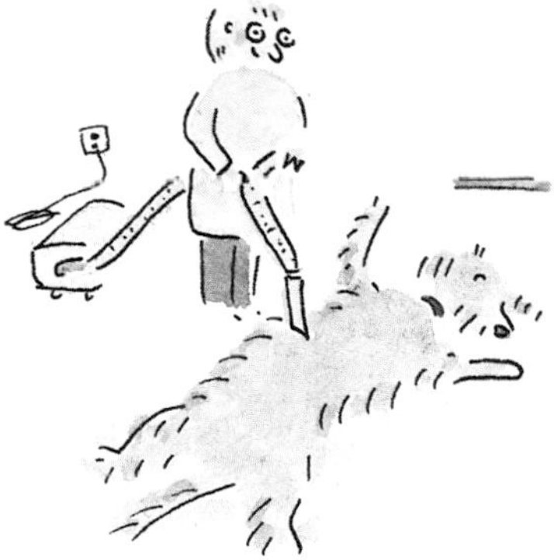

THERE are TIMES WHEN I PRETEND MY DOG'S

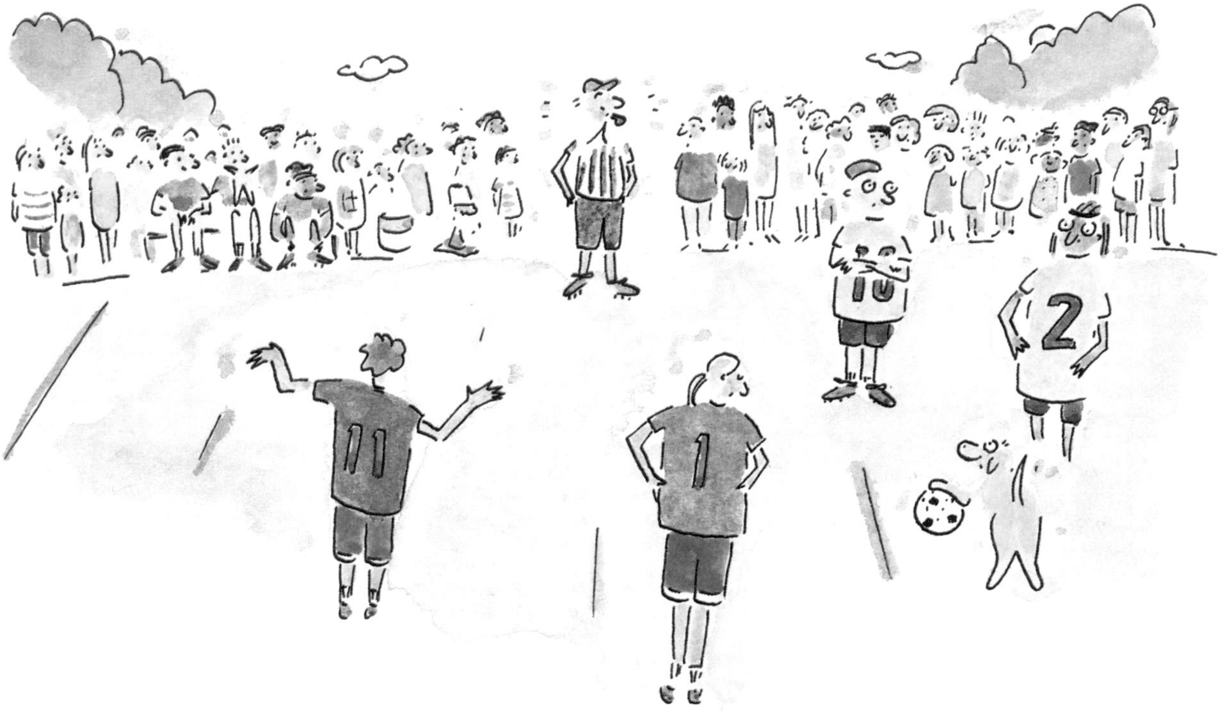
10
2
11
1

not MY DOG . . .

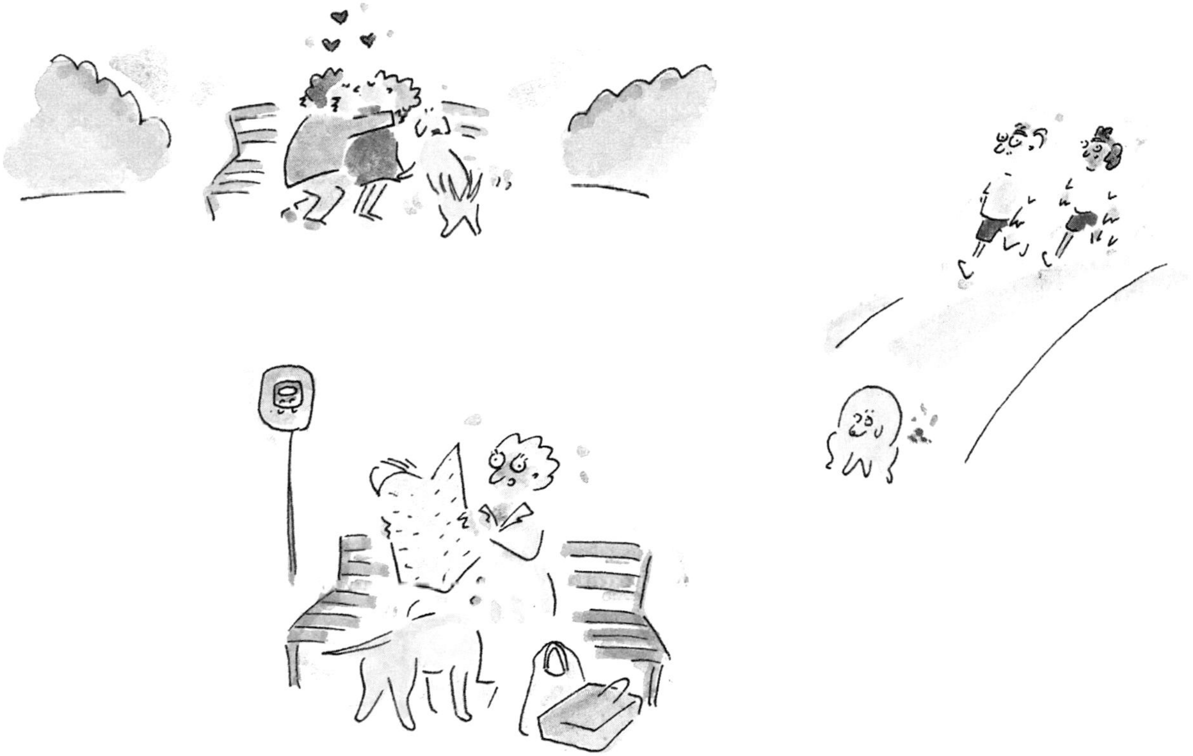

BUT THEN I REMIND MYSELF OF ALL THE THINGS I WOULDN'T DO

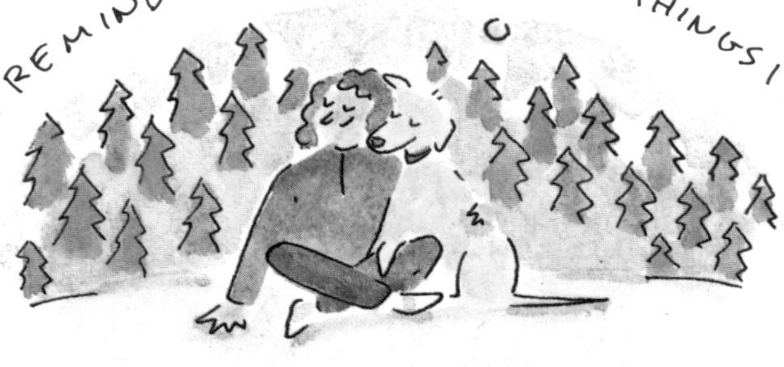

IF IT WEREN'T FOR MY DOG.

I WOULDN'T NECESSARILY GET OUT OF BED EVERY DAY.
I WOULDN'T GO TO THE WOODS EVERY DAY OR RUN
ON THE ROADS EVERY DAY. I WOULDN'T FIND SOMETHING
NEW EVERY DAY, SEE ALL THE DEER, SMELL ALL THE
SMELLS OR SING ALL THE SONGS 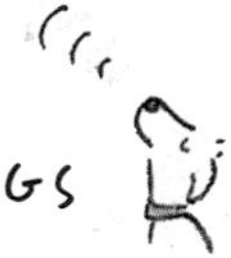 AT THE TOP OF MY LUNGS.
I WOULDN'T FEEL THE WIND BY MY EARS OR WALK IN
THE RAIN. I WOULDN'T GET TO KNOW ALL OF THE
PEOPLE 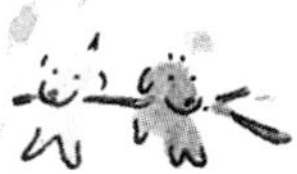 AND ALL OF THEIR DOGS. 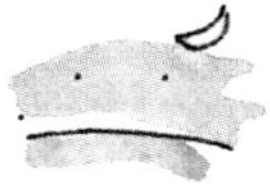

I LIKE HOW SHE CAN MOVE HER NOSE WITHOUT MOVING HER HEAD.

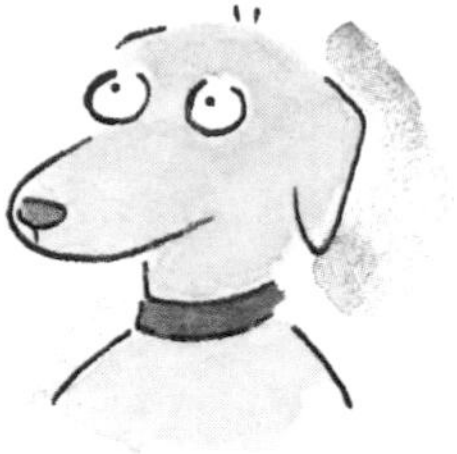

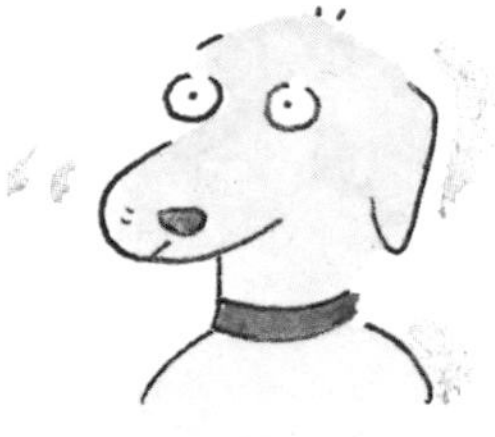

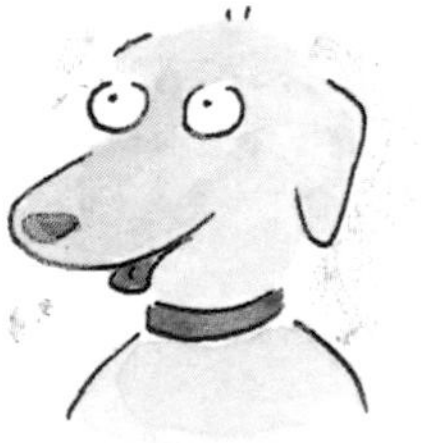

At ease.

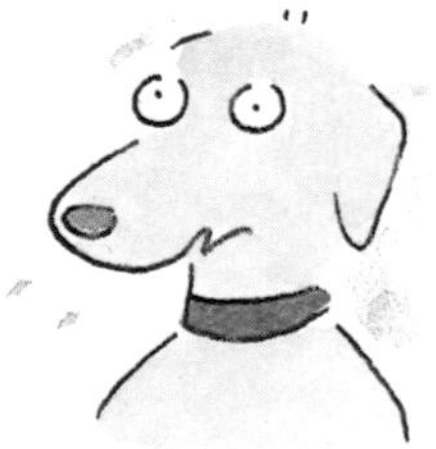

At·tention!

OR SOMETIMES WHEN HER LIP GETS STUCK ON HER TEETH.

SHE SMILES

when she's just about to throw up
or sometimes when she's scratching.

SHE'S RIGHT THERE WHEN I'M HAPPY

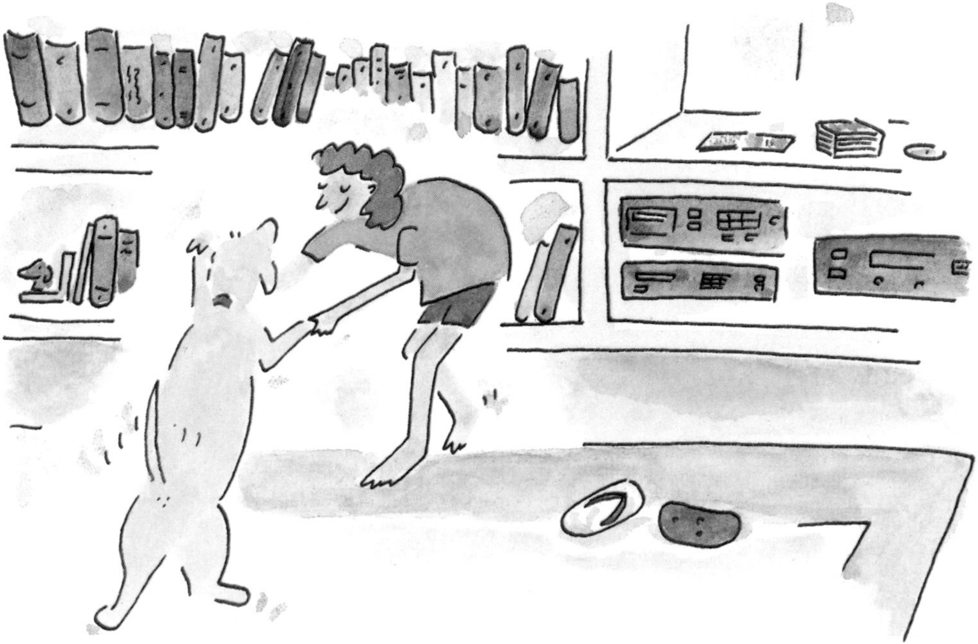

or sad.

I LOVE THIS DOG
THE BEST
IN THE WORLD.

She's the World's Best Dog.

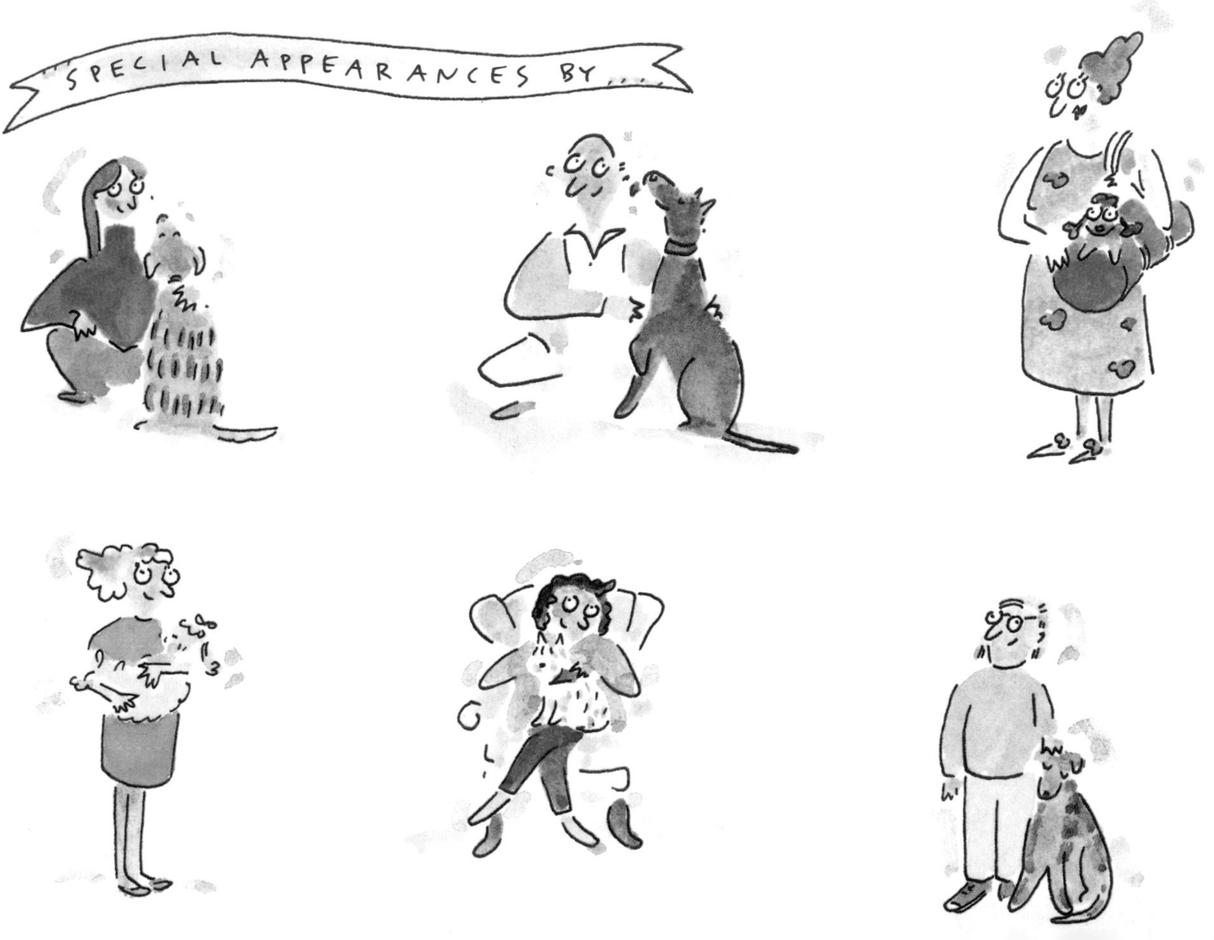
SPECIAL APPEARANCES BY ....

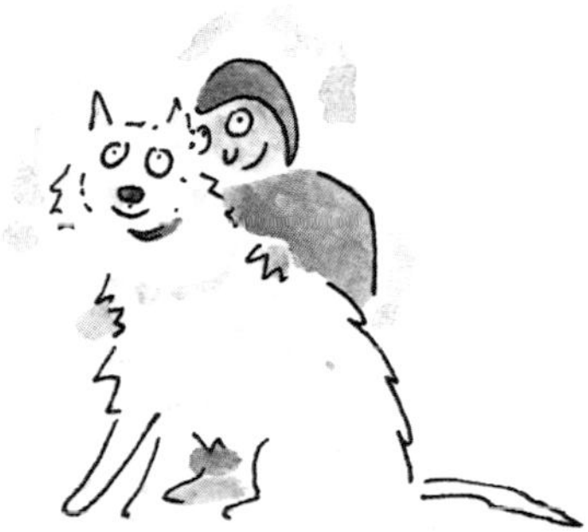

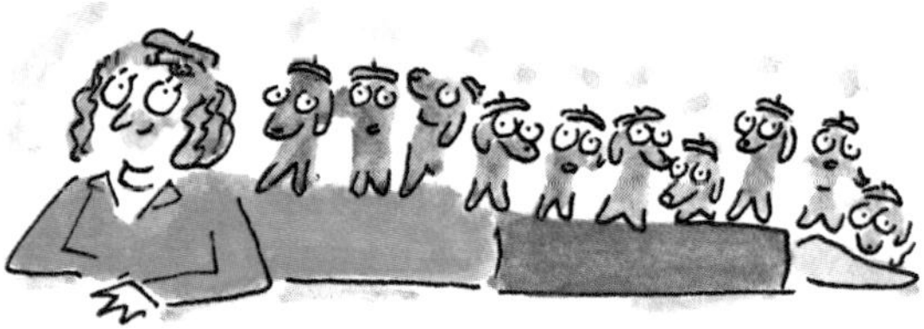

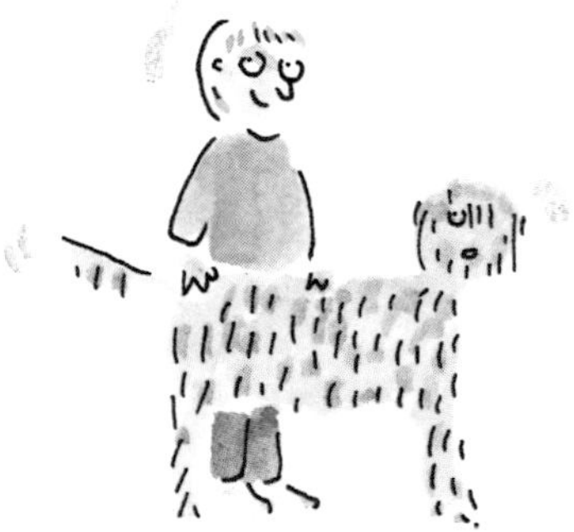

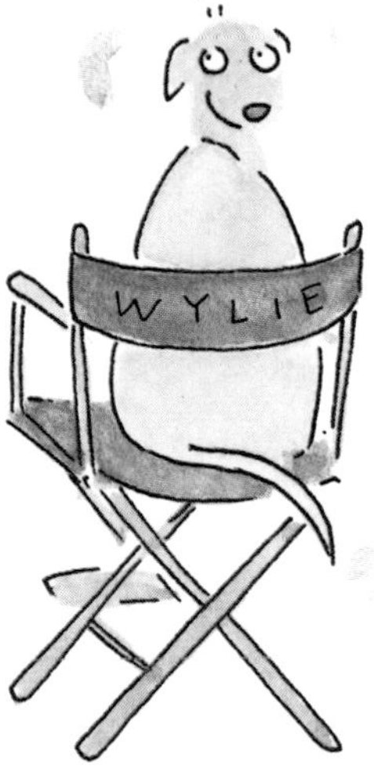
WYLIE

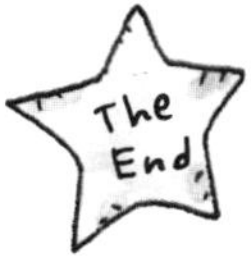
The
End

ABOUT THE AUTHOR

In addition to writing about dogs and cats, Suzy Becker created *The All Better Book*, an illustrated anthology of kids' solutions to world problems. She has also been a White House Fellow, a greeting card entrepreneur, an organizer of bicycle rides for AIDS and, currently, a teacher at the Francis W. Parker Charter Essential School in central Massachusetts. Wylie joins her on business trips; Binky stays home in the sunny spots. And yes, that's really Suzy's handwriting in the books.